I feel BAD ABOUT my DICK

LAMENTATIONS
OF
MASCULINE
VANITY
AND
LISTS OF
STARTLING
PERTINENCE

by

DARRYL PONICSÁN

PLEASUREBOATSTUDIO
A NONPROFIT LITERARY PRESS

Hardback ISBN 978-0-912887-91-3
Paperback ISBN 978-0-912887-92-0
Library of Congress Control Number:
2019952993

Cover and book Design by Lauren Grosskopf

Pleasure Boat Studio books are available through your favorite bookstore and through the following:
SPD (Small Press Distribution) 800-869-7553
Baker & Taylor 800-775-1100
Ingram 615-793-5000
Amazon.com and bn.com

& through
PLEASURE BOAT STUDIO: A NONPROFIT LITERARY PRESS
WWW.PLEASUREBOATSTUDIO.COM
Seattle, Washington

Also by DARRYL PONICSÁN

NOVELS

Eternal Sojourners
The Last Detail
Goldengrove
Andoshen, Pa.
Cinderella Liberty
The Accomplice
Tom Mix Died For You Sins
The Ringmaster
An Unmarried Man
Last Flag Flying

AS ANNE ARGULA

Homicide My Own
Walla Walla Suite
Krapp's Last Cassette
The Other Romanian

TELEVISION

The Mississippi (Series, created by)
A Girl Called Hatter Fox (movie of the week)
The Enemy Within (HBO movie)

SCREENPLAYS

Cinderella Liberty
Taps (with two other dudes)
VisionQuest
The Boost
Nuts (with two other dudes)
School Ties (with another dude)
Random Hearts (with another dude)
Last Flag Flying (with another dude)

I FEEL BAD ABOUT MY DICK

TABLE OF CONTENTS

PREFACE / DEDICATION

Several years ago, whilst perusing the used books at a library sale, it occurred to me that without James Patterson and his assembly line there would be little to sell. I was there to find coffee-table art books originally costing $100 marked down to $2, my kind of discount. I also shop used-book sales for hardcovers I wouldn't read outside of solitary confinement because they make interesting surfaces for pastels and prints.

I don't save books as I used to. Right out of college, the first thing I did in any new hovel was to construct bookshelves out of cinder blocks and planks and fill them with my books, randomly arranged. It was a way of telling whoever came inside, "This is me." Now whoever comes inside has to find out for herself. I still keep a hundred or so copies of first editions and books inscribed by their authors, some of whom were friends or acquaintances. This is not to say I can't be seduced by a trim little number with a cute cover.

Those of us who love books talk about the sensuous experience of approaching a new one, the pleasure of running our fingertips over the face of it, the flush of anticipation, and then, yes, opening it, smelling it, and turning the first page, keeping our left index finger under the page as we read, slowly, savoring the language if it's good and moving that finger, yes, stroking the underside or teasing with little bounces while the thumb of the other hand holds down the opposite side of the book with fingers firmly against the backside of the cover, over the picture of the author, which we save for later, and then, yes, spending the night with it, yes, and falling asleep with it in our arms, satisfied. Smoke?

Anyway, a book by Nora Ephron caught my eye. *I Feel Bad About My Neck.* I knew of the author and had enjoyed her movies. The book was promoted as "wry, amusing, marvelous." Usually I would have moved on at "marvelous," a description I've never trusted about anything, and one that makes me not want to stand too close to whoever is uttering the word. It's much like "awesome" at the other end of the social scale. The book, I read, had been on *The New York Times* Best Seller List, which should be a warning instead of an affirmation if you've been burned more than once by the books on *The New York Times* Best Seller List. The reason these books are on the best seller list is that everyone is reading them. The same could be said about watching the Kardashians.

I stood in the windmill of elbows snatching up bargains, the bright yellow paperback in hand. Why would a woman feel bad about her neck? Why keep looking at your neck in the mirror if it makes you feel bad? Is it the male-gaze thing? (Which is itself one more thing I've never understood.) It started, I think, with how women were viewed in movies. Dudes would not mind having the thing reversed: gaze all you want. The male gaze isn't much different than the female gaze. Women look at other women the same way dudes do, without the accompanying fantasy, perhaps, and more often down the nose.

So the neck thing. I've never heard any man or woman make a comment about someone else's neck, unless it was grotesquely inked. ("My God, she's got a zipper tattooed around her neck! It's partway open! Something's trying to crawl out!") Can you say the same about a dick? You feel bad about your neck, Nora? I'll see your neck and raise you a dick, if a dick I can raise.

I tossed the book back into the bin and browsed in other genres, but I was inexplicably drawn back to it. I was curious about someone who feels bad about her neck. The book had the virtue of being low-slung, a one-seater, and I had nothing going on that afternoon except a bottle of Ram's Gate chardonnay chilling in an ice bucket. I paid my dollar and went home to read the book.

Once finished, I didn't know what to make of it, and it wasn't because the bottle of wine was now empty. Miss Ephron, I thought, was all about things being delivered to her and worrying about how she looked to the world, how she cooked and parented and lived and everything like that. In her book written for older women she pointed out with no irony that *"There are all sorts of books written for older women...I find these books utterly useless."*

Brady T. Brady, to whom this book is dedicated, is a literate friend of mine who makes other pessimists appear, if not cheery, at least hopeful by comparison. I told him I had a gift for him and tossed the book across his desk. He looked at the title, then up at me. He said, "Yeah, and I feel bad about my dick."

The rest, as they say, is sophistry.

I went to work on drawing a parallel between women's necks and the dicks of dudes. But then Nora died and the fun went out of it. The moment of respectful silence stretched into several years, which in the life of a writer is looked back upon as no more than a lost weekend. A day came when I shuffled through some old notes, as writers always do, pruning the branches that were never going to bear fruit, I came upon a list of possible chapters I might write (See also "Chapters That Did Not Make the Cut") if I were to write a dude's answer to Nora's lament.

I get it that as a woman ages she comes to worry about things she never thought she would. She worries about what she shows to the world: cellulite, thinning lips, expanding thighs, parts of her that jiggle when she dances, and, why not, the neck. If a dude worries at all it's about the stuff no one sees: the prostate, the heart, the pancreas, parts of him that hurt when he hurls, and, for sure, the dick.

I decided to have another run at it, and here we are. As Nora's book at times veers into some serious territory, there is a risk that this one will, too, but it will all come out okay in the end.

During the ten years it took from having the idea to writing the book, I moved around a bit, which accounts for why this stuff does not appear to be chronological. When I write, for example, *I live in Seattle*, I may or may not, but once I did. When I write that I moved to the desert, be assured that I did, but I may not live there now, regardless of what it says under, "About the Author." Though out of order, everything in this book is the truth, the whale truth, and nodding but the truth.

I feel BAD ABOUT my DICK

If I were to say to you, "I feel bad about my dick," (and there I have) and you are a woman, you would laugh and spit up your Lemon Drop. I know this to be true. A dude, however, would squint and say, "What's up with that?" and he would want to hear every last detail. Sorrow or shame? Guilt? Burden? Physical or mental? Recent or always? Is it the age thing? Is it the curve or the color? Is it hooded? Does it pale by comparisons? At rest or ready for business? A dude will ask all that and more, because he feels bad about his own dick. Thus, the difference between men and women. Others may exist.

A man's experience with his dick begins when he has it in his power to make his hands go wherever he wants them to go. Fairly early in life. Years pass and he arrives at an age when only his urologist has any interest in the thing. (And one has to ask the good doctor, why choose that particular specialty?)

When I'm with my drinking friends—who are not actual friends, since I don't even know their last names; most of them, I don't even know their *first* names, some of them, like back in the Pennsylvania coal regions where my boyhood pals were Chewie, Lemonears, Wheezer, and Shovel, and I myself was known as Li'l Monk because my older brother was Big Monk—I look at them and wonder why they wear baseball caps or team jerseys with a player's name on the back. (Which in my case is "Pence" because when Hunter Pence first came to the Giants he couldn't hit and he couldn't field and he looked like a newly discovered avian species. I bad-mouthed him without mercy. When finally he caught fire and became the heart of the team, I felt obliged to wear his jersey as a penance.) My drinking buddies no longer have the knees to play sports themselves. (They feel bad about their knees; see "Chapters That Did Not Make the Cut.") They've become barroom jocks watching the game with one eye and scratch tickets with the other, usually through the top half of one bifocal and the bottom half of another, well aware of the huge contracts these players have earned for dazzling us with incredible plays while disgusting us with stupid mistakes we ourselves could make as stupidly and for far less money.

Why do dudes preoccupy themselves with sports they can no longer play and long shots they know they can't win? Because they feel bad about their dicks. Not long enough, thick enough, or, when called upon, hard enough. Too scrawny or flabby, or lazy. Some look downright scary, all blue and threatening like a cop, or puny and pale as a gin-and-tonic. We know they're not pretty. Even we don't like to look at them, ours or anyone else's, though because we are dudes we are thrown into so many situations where we can't avoid it: locker rooms, communal showers, stadium piss troughs, the USS Monrovia (APA-31). Some dicks act like stumblebums you don't want to believe are on your team. They won't listen up no matter who's calling the plays, and they trip over themselves at the worst possible moments. You can't depend on them in clutch situations like long relief or overtime. It's why you call someone who does rude or stupid things a dick.

One of the euphemisms for a dick (which is itself a euphemism) is "member." Member of what? Who sponsored Dick for the club?

The late Carlos Castaneda, a famous anthropologist and visionary who was a close friend back in the day, used to go on and on about the vagina, what an incredible thing it was, a dreamcatcher, a source of stupendous power. ("Stupendous" was one of his favorite words. He pushed it through his projecting lips like a shot.) Much in the world was stupendous to Carlos but nothing came close to the warm moist vagina. He surrounded himself with women, mostly sorceresses, one of whom was a reedy quiet soul with a black belt in a particularly lethal school of karate. Men, Carlos lectured, plod through their lives with an albatross hanging not from their necks like the Ancient Mariner but between their legs, like a Peruvian pot.

If you've seen one vagina you've pretty much seen them all. All that differs is the sweep of the fur, if any, and the presence of a piercing. Not so with dicks. Like fingerprints, no two are alike. From Michelangelo's "David" to Mapplethorpe's "Man in a Polyester Suit," the visual range of dicks is all but infinite, and that's before any discussion on the spectrum of personalities inherent in Dick A through Z.

According to my urologist, Dr. Dark, the dick is destined for a downward slide sooner than any dude anticipates, and you're sliding right behind it. You can grow a beard, wear a rug, work out in smelly gyms, buy a Hummer, pack a Glock where it's permitted, which is damn near everywhere, but there's nothing you can do about a disinterested dick that's not much to look at. Not surgery—and who would? (Women, apparently, who don't think twice about getting a surgeon to go all up in there and recreate the peach of a sixteen-year-old.) Nor other medical intervention, though an avalanche of emails shout *"Au contraire, mon frére!"* Delete them as soon as you get them. It is what it is and was what it was and will be what it was. (It should be noted that the first dick transplant—not an elective surgery, by the way—has already occurred, a fifteen-hour medical marvel performed over two days. Little-known fact: this first recorded dick transplant was in fact the second, because the very first transplant was rejected, not by the host body to which it was attached but by the dude's wife, who could not bear dealing with a strange dick. At least that's what she said, and the dude honored her horror. True love.)

Dudes deal with the downward drift by ignoring it, the bedrock of the male code. Go with low-wattage in the bathroom. Lose the mirrors. Most dudes will at some point in their lives have a mirrored wall in the bedroom and will enjoy the reflection of their performance. Women, not so much. Women offer us the view, because we seem to like it so much. Women, if they peek at all, see only the parts that are jiggling, so they look the other way. For that matter, I am not watching my reflection because I'm some Adonis. I watch because the reflections are undeniable proof that this is really happening. Which probably accounts for amateur sex tapes, permanent records of romantic fulfillment. The girls I dated, however, were too smart to fall for "It'll be just for the two of us."

Back when I said something about baseball? I meant to say more about sportswear. I could do a couple of pages about grown men wearing baseball caps backwards or, worse, sideways, but let us observe for an uncomfortable moment, sweatpants. Let us accept sweatpants as either a rebellious breach of fashion or a display of utter disregard for one's appearance. Their only redeeming asset is the absence of a zipper. When the occasion demands more than sweatpants and you don a pair of Balmain jeans, $1,375 a clatter, distressed to create the illusion of what a dude who works under his car might wear, and upon arriving have to go to the men's room, remember that this is no time for an accident involving a zipper, though I'd be hard pressed to name a time when it would be appropriate. The advice is simple: don't rush, even if you are in a hurry. Dudes have a tendency to rush every process of life, from eating a Philly cheesesteak sandwich to having sex, and that includes standing at a urinal, especially standing at a urinal, and trying to avoid a quick glance at the next guy's sad dick or letting him cop a look at theirs. A rush to leak the lizard can lead to medical problems, according to Dr. Dark. For one thing, it provides an environment for the formation of crystals, and like the fortune teller's crystal ball could foretell an unhappy future. A dude must try to empty the bladder even as it becomes more difficult with age. In the time it takes an old dude to finish, standing there in someone else's puddle, two young dudes have come and gone, and he's still singing, *"Nobody gonna slow me down, oh no, I got to keep on peeing."* Once done, and with the awareness of a Zen master, a dude is wise to tuck it securely away before zipping up.

My Norwegian friend Odd and I were sitting with all four elbows on the bar, watching the hapless Mariners on TV, when Odd said, "Some sorry shit this morning, you know."

Said I: "What was that?"

"I woke up with an erection there. First one since I can't remember."

"What's so terrible about that?"

"Both my hands were asleep."

One more example of how a dick will sabotage another

part of your anatomy, and a regretful reminder to me that not only did I not get enough sex when I was young—it was the Eisenhower era—I did not even spend enough quality time alone with "Little Donald." (An unfortunate moniker given the path of presidential history. Oh, come on, everybody gives it a name. Women name their cars Bruce; dudes name their dicks Little Something or other.)

More often than not, over the course of this impossible mission called life, "Little Donny" has been the rogue agent out of step with headquarters and all the cells in the field. To push the geopolitical metaphor one click further, in the world that is a dude, his dick is Cuba. Defiant, obstinate, an agenda all its own. You can barricade it, starve it, isolate it, slap it around, and it will still laugh in your face—or at your toes—and fire up a Cohiba and dance along the Malecón. We sputter on about North Korea and Iran, we wring our hands over Iraq and Syria, but at the end of the day what gets to us is that little strip of land below our belt that we aren't even allowed to visit, lest it be seen as support. So next time you hear a girl say, "You're such a dick," think of Cuba. (Or now that I've provided the metaphor, try *not* to think of Cuba.)

Now, I've been around. I've been to fifty-seven county fairs and Cuba more than once. I've been up and down, rich and poor, in pain and joy. I've found love and lost love and found it again in a windy place, and watched it blow away again, only to have it jump on my back at the most inappropriate time. I've seen foul treachery and touching loyalty. (I've seen fire and I've seen rain.) I've seen more and more war and not enough peace. After all that I am here to tell you what matters most in life. My dick.

CEREAL *TOPOGRAPHY*

I would be thinner today were it not for *Woman's Day*. As a young man I had no interest in food. Some dudes lived to eat; I ate to live. Skinny as a swami. I had no experience of eating as a social event because my people didn't see it that way, and once on my own I was too poor to dine out.

Often, involved in some task, usually writing, I would forget to eat. I had but one meal in my cooking repertoire: ground beef, chopped peppers and onions, fried up together, lots of ketchup added for the last few minutes of cooking. (Where I grew up in Pennsylvania, by the way, peppers were called mangoes for reasons I never learned. I was twenty-seven and in California before I discovered a fruit by that name existed and consuming it was an art that had to be learned with a California girl sitting on your lap. Ditto for artichokes.) Only so much of that kind of fry-up can be consumed without causing depression, but I did not know how to make anything else.

Then one day in the mail came a cookbook, sent to me by the good people of *Woman's Day*, probably because they thought Darryl was a woman's name. (See "I Feel Funny Telling Colored Girls My Name is Darryl, Part One"). The book was complimentary. If I did nothing, they would send me the other eleven volumes in the set at a reduced price, which eventually they did because I had by that time some expertise in doing nothing.

As soon as the rest of the set arrived, I paged through all twelve volumes. The photos knocked me out. Sitting outside on a hot January day in Los Angeles, I found myself newly interested in cuisine. I salivated over the images of a table set with a New England-style boiled dinner, oysters baked in their shells, and Boston cream pie. I wanted to eat everything I saw. I read the accompanying recipes and thought, I can do that. How tough can it be? (*How tough can it be* is another masculine mantra and accounts for why dudes often have fewer fingers than women and why they wind up electrocuted in greater numbers.)

I made up my mind that whatever the cost of this set of cookbooks, I would pay it, even if I had to borrow the money. I would teach myself to cook from these volumes and never go hungry again, as Dog is my witness. (See Chapter Thirty-five, "As Dog is My Witness.") As it happened, the billing department overlooked invoicing me and I never reminded them, so, *Woman's Day*, I owe you. I own the well-worn set to this day and have carried it through two marriages and numerous changes of address. It's my go-to resource. The only good advice I ever gave my son was, "If you can read, you can cook," which is true, though it will never get you past the early auditions for Master Chef. One might reasonably hope, however, it gets you a third date and all due respect, because nothing attracts a woman more than a dude who can whip up a loving meal, present it in a civilized fashion, and pair it with the right pinot noir at the end of her hard day.

As for me, I had always assumed that my mother or someone like her would be around to make a meal for me, and it worked out that way all through college. Then, living alone in my first hovel, I was left to my own devices. I weighed in at about one-thirty and was six-foot-one, hardly casting a shadow, and when I had to eat I did it in grim places that used to be something else before they became restaurants, like failed mortuaries, or at bars that sold smoked carp with pretzels. This was before fast-food joints, when you had to go inside and sit down and take as long as it took. If I continued to eat out, even at this modest level, I would wind up spending my entire pittance of a high-school teacher's salary, $4,500 a year, on my hovel and preserving what little meat I had on my bones.

That is when and why I came up with my one-pan meal, which I ate every day and which would occasionally make me feel bad about my ability to live without a mother around. It never occurred to me that I could have found someone, maybe even my mother, to teach me how to cook. If I thought of it at all, I thought of cooking like playing the clarinet. It was too late for me.

I was living in Owego at the time, a cheerless gray river town in upstate New York. One day I was pushing my cart through the market, dropping into it a green mango (bell pepper), an onion, and a pound of ground beef, when an item on a lower shelf caught my eye. Tortillas! This was in 1961 and no Mexican had yet found his way to Owego. I had never met one but I thought of all Mexicans as exotic. (Eighteen years later I would marry one. Lucky for me, she thought Jews were exotic. Luckier still, she thought I was a Jew. [I haven't told her otherwise.]) All I knew about tortillas was that they were Mexican food, and that was all I needed to know. They came packaged ten in a round sealed can around two inches thick, believe it or not. I did not know enough then to question that packaging. I threw a can into my cart and rushed to the checkout line.

I sped back to the hovel and opened the can. There they were, wrapped in paper. Tortillas! All the imagined romance of south of the border flooded over me. Beautiful señoritas. Heartbreaking mariachi music. Recalcitrant burros. Fiery tequila! No directions were provided, and in those days they didn't list ingredients on the package. The less you knew the better, was the ethos. I had no clue how tortillas were made, what they were made of, or what you were supposed to do with them. I thought of frying them up with my signature dish, but that felt wrong. (It would have been more right than what followed.) Instead, I set the oven for 375 degrees and spread all ten of the tortillas on the racks, nervous over my first attempt at Mexican food.

Every five minutes or so I looked in on them, but nothing was happening. After twenty minutes I turned off the oven and took them out. It was now or never. Of course they were rock-hard and inedible. The mariachi music in my head faded away with a mournful cry.

My hovel was on the second floor. I opened the window and one by one I threw the tortillas like Frisbees toward the Susquehanna River. They landed I know not where.

Four years later, I drove alone across the country. Upon arriving in Los Angeles at dusk, my first stop was at a Mexican food stand on Pico Boulevard. I looked at the menu board, a stranger in a strange land. I recognized nothing beyond Coke. "I'll have a take-o," I said. The people behind the window laughed.

I squirreled my take-o back to my TR-3 and bit into it, sending bits of lettuce and drops of salsa over my lap. I loved it! Mexican food! City of Angels!

POSTSCRIPT:

My Exotic Wife and I dine together when we go out to restaurants, a few nights a week. We seldom, however, share a meal together at home. She cannot bear to see an egg frying first thing in the morning, and the smell of food before noon puts her off. She escapes the kitchen area and waits for me to make my own fried eggs, each corralled inside a large onion ring, with tater tots and maybe a few slices of Spam, yelling at a distance to please, please, please turn on the fans. Creamed chipped beef on toast ("Shit on a shingle" if you're a military vet) is another of my specialties, as is chorizo con huevos, which my E.W. should be making for me but so far has not. (I get on her nerves by claiming that after years in California I am more Mexican than she, even though she can better communicate in Spanish, while all I can do is correct her grammar. Putting that gripe aside, when she does make her enchiladas I swoon to the floor and she has to step over me.)

I eat breakfast alone, playing Words With Friends. I've spent most of my professional life sitting alone, which sounds worse than it is, so eating alone does not make me feel bad. She will come into the kitchen when the coast is clear and mix fruit into a large bowl of yogurt and call it a meal. She forgets to eat lunch, as I sometimes do myself, but when she does, it is an encore of breakfast. For me, on the other hand, it's a mortadella and cheese sandwich, dill pickle, and a handful of potato chips on the side. Dinner is where I shine. I'll cook giant casseroles—rice, noodles, or potatoes mixed with leftover pork, chicken, ground beef or canned tuna. Cheese, of course. Mushroom soup probably. I'll eat it for three successive dinners and freeze the rest, defrost it in a month, then eat it for another three successive dinners. E.W. will have avocado toast, sometimes with scrambled eggs, which she finds tolerable in the evening. I can entice her with my paella, which is pretty damn good, and a great Caesar salad, which I learned how to assemble at Caesar's in Tijuana, where it was invented.

Mostly, though, in the area of food we come together in restaurants. (I have no problem eating alone in restaurants either, me and a book. One of the many things I love about Paris is how a table for one is so easily accepted.) We often eat out with family or friends, during which I can enjoy myself or not. I don't like people wanting a bit of something off my plate, and I don't ever want anything off theirs, though they might try to force it on me. ("You have to try this." "No, I don"t.") There ought to be an alternative to eating as the means to social intercourse. Drinking works better for me.

IT'S *my* HEAD *and* *I'll* WEAR *a* BERET *IF I WANT TO*

Between my misadventure with canned tortillas and my sneaking into Los Angeles under the cover of darkness a period of some four or five years passed, during which I dropped out of graduate school to join the Navy and then dropped out of the Navy to go back to graduate school. Armed with my newly minted MA degree from Cornell I set out on my beater Triumph TR-3 and headed west. I had two hundred dollars saved from substitute teaching at Ithaca High, no credit cards, and few well-wishers. My own father predicted that I would break down on the desert and die of thirst. "You'll get bit by a snake," my mother added.

I took my father's warning more seriously. The TR-3 was never reliable and it was more than likely I would break down somewhere. I could only hope it wouldn't be in the middle of a desert, surrounded by snakes. I made up my mind that should the car break down, wherever that might be, that would be where I start my new life. I would find a teaching job and chalk it up to British manufacturing.

The first leg of my journey ended in New Concord, Ohio, 382 miles from my starting point in Pennsylvania. I spent $12.15 that day. $1.75 for the turnpike toll, $1.50 on food, $2.90 cents on gas, and $6 for a motel. I can cite these figures after so many years because I wrote them down at the end of each day. (I did not write anything about the scenery or the people I may have encountered along the way, like the cop who stopped me early one morning on a lonely stretch of road in the panhandle of Texas because I was wearing a beret. I cannot remember our conversation, but it did not end in a Texas jail.) The second day of the journey, I reached Vandalia, Illinois, cost $14.80, but that included $1.50 for "Grease," which means I must have stopped at a station for a lube job because the musical had not yet been written. The entire trip, 2,767 miles, took me seven days, at a total cost of $104.75, which meant I rolled into Hollywood with $95.25 in my pocket.

The TR-3 held up. The desert did not defeat me, no snake bit me, but there were moments when I silently prayed, *"Not here. Please, don't make me start a life here."* Places like Miami, the one in Oklahoma. Please not Amarillo, Texas, or the two hundred miles of wilderness on either side of it. You can stick Gallup, New Mexico, too, though upon driving through the Land of Enchantment I found that the majesty of the rock formations made me aware in the moment. They seemed capable of speech, but the only rock I was conversant with was anthracite coal. I drove conscientiously, trying to cross the overwhelming expanse, past the looming rocks, without calling attention to myself, which certainly I might have, since at least one cop thought I bore looking into, both because of the beret I was shamelessly wearing and the appearance of the car I was willfully driving, which I will get into later.

POSTSCRIPT:

I scold my younger self for driving across the country—five times, in fact—and recording only expenses. I know writers are supposed to keep journals so that no precious thought goes unpreserved, and I tried a few times but gave it up after a week or so. I equate it with taking pictures, another thing I don't do. If I come upon a picture of myself taken twenty years ago and I feel bad about it—maybe I was wearing shorts—I can't throw it out, because destroying pictures is bad ju-ju. (Is it even possible now to throw out pictures? Does "delete" mean what it used to?) It's the same with journals, but I'll take on the ju-ju debt to burn an old diary because it doesn't mean anything to anyone, including me. Some of the stuff I wrote and published in college is out of my control, yellowing in attics all over the country, and I feel bad about that.

What makes it worse is that people are always giving me little Moleskine notebooks because that's how Hemingway took notes, which could be true, but why should I? Even if Hemingway is a good role model for a writer (See "I Feel Bad About My Role Models") at some point you have to let him go, and the Moleskine notebook may be a good place to start. If I don't want to forget something I will write it down on whatever scrap of paper is at hand, and then later put it in a drawer. If and when I use whatever I wrote on it, I'll toss it. When I leave the house I carry a sketchbook in my murse. As I flip through it now I see more notes than sketches but nothing that would constitute a journal. I have the name of a dude who demonstrates some back exercises on YouTube. I have a couple half-finished songs I'm writing for the ukulele, a list of anti-inflammatory foods, the titles of some books I want to read, and this: *"She promised me some work-out tits but when I got there all she did was show me how to exercise."*

Things I FOUND OUT for MYSELF, SOONER OR LATER

(Part One)

Always split eights

Don't buy, rent

Don't rent, borrow

Salt, yes; sugar, no

The last four years of junior college are a waste

Drink the good stuff first

Don't take naked selfies

Ten percent of $100 is $7.25

A hide-a-bed is a bad purchase

Always order doubles

When someone says, "It's not the money," it is the money

Whenever a man says, "Believe me," don't believe him

You can't try on underwear before you buy it

Don't wrestle with a decision before you have to step into the ring

Caution always, fear never

Don't take a cell phone to the toilet

Dog is always right

Improv is more fun for those doing it than for those watching it

If less is more then nothing is everything

When you are alone, act as though a crowd is watching you

When a crowd is watching you, act as though you are alone

It can always get worse

I feel BAD ABOUT my MURSE

It is not so much that I hate my murse, it is that I must carry one at all. Was a time I could carry all that I needed in my pockets, but as time went on the stuff I needed to carry multiplied. Here is what I need now whenever I leave the house: iPhone, sanitizing wipes, Altoids, penlight, Palomino Blackwing pencil, stylus, Mount Blanc fountain pen, Black Mountain leather sketch book with a hundred-dollar bill tucked in there somewhere, Think Thin high-protein bar, and Ibuprofens.

But wait, there's more. A French-made knife, two pairs of glasses, car keys for my keyless Nissan, loyalty cards for Ralph's, True Value, B-12 shots, and the Regal Theater, Toyota ear buds, homeopathic cough drops, and whatever else I might need for any particular urban expedition. That's in addition to what I still carry in my pockets: wallet, hankie, house keys, change, a Japanese-made knife, and some sort of talisman. (The knives are for opening things. *All* things. Anxiety over tampering has imposed a security on ordinary products tantamount to Jodie Foster's first interview with Hannibal Lecter. I used to be up to fighting my way out of a biker bar. Now I can't open a bag of chips without a sharp knife. Some blister packaging requires a heavy-duty wire snippers.)

Not all dudes carry murses, for fear of appearing unmanly, which means the great majority of dudes don't want to be seen near one. I see young dudes out and about in black T-shirts and skinny jeans, which was David Duchovny's entire wardrobe for *Californication.* I don't know how they do it. (Yes, I do, now that I think of it. The flashlight is in the phone. No need for notebooks, pen, or pencil, because there's an app for that. They pay with their phone, no need for cash. Their loyalty cards are on the phone or they have renounced loyalty, something I'm thinking of doing myself. Their eyesight is 20-20. They're unconcerned about germs, trusting in their own immune systems. Most of what I have to carry could be condensed into an iPhone, if I had the kind of brain that works that way, which I don't. The iPhone is just one more thing I have to carry.)

My murse is about the size of David Foster Wallace's *Infinite Jest.* (It can be argued that reading that book, cover to cover, is almost as great an achievement as having written it.) My murse has no label or designer logo. I suspect it was handmade by a leather craftsman and sold originally at a street fair. I bought it forty-odd years ago at a friend's garage sale, for two dollars. This friend was ten years older than I and he had owned it long enough to want to get rid of it. I did not carry it regularly until I moved to Palm Springs, where it doesn't matter if you carry a murse or not: you're still going to be perceived as gay. The leather is brown and distressed, but anything over fifty years old is going to be a little brown and distressed (like a dick). It has outside compartments for one set of glasses and two writing instruments. It has eight slots for cards and a slot for your checkbook. Behind the slots is a place for hiding another hundred-dollar bill. All of that is on the outside, under a flap. The inside always surprises me by how much I can stuff into it. It's quite a production.

An anti-murse dude might point out that I could wear

cargo pants and dispense with the girlie accessory. Given a choice between cargo pants, or God forbid, cargo shorts, I'll take the murse. (I'll take two murses.) No way you can wear cargo pants and not look like a dick. (Nora Ephron, I'm sure, would never have worn cargo pants. I've never seen any woman wear them.)

The murse stays in the picture.

I LOVE LA

You might wonder how, even in 1965, a dude could roll into LA with three gallons of gas left in the tank and $95.25 in cash and coin, and not wind up having to do some pretty unsavory stuff to stay there. Fortunately I had a friend named Manzo who had moved to Los Angeles from New York the year before and it was he who urged me to relocate from the East Coast. He called LA a "great hick town." I could stay with him, he said, until I got a foothold. He was a jazz saxophonist and singer working in juvenile detention. He advised me to take the civil-service exam, as he had, and work for the county, as he was, until I could write a book and he could get a record contract. Even so, I had to sell some of what little I had and borrow the rest to get over the hump. It was mid-summer and schools had already staffed their faculties. I was not sure I wanted to return to teaching anyway. I aced the civil-service exam and was offered a job as a social worker, OAA, Old Age Assistance. A three-week orientation and training period preceded my taking it to the streets but I was soon making calls on clients in the same beater TR-3 that brought me across the country.

Manzo lived in a three-story rooming house on Washington Boulevard, in a black neighborhood. The room was big enough for both of us, bathroom down the hall, though we had to share a bed. Shortly after I started my gig as a social worker and was learning my way around town, the Watts

Riot erupted. Not that Rodney King exercise, but The Big One. Mayhem in the streets, blood in the heart, bullets in the air, Molotov cocktails rolling around in the trunk. We lived within the curfew area, which was cool for Manzo because he was black. I was on the blond side. I'd been nothing but comfortable moving around the 'hood, but Manzo told me I ought to make myself scarce for awhile until the smoke cleared. Before I tell you about all that, however, I have to back up to that TR-3, which stays in my memory like a bad happenstance.

I traded sideways for it, giving up a '55 Ford hardtop Crown Victoria, a responsive and dependable beauty, which if it's still around is worth twentyfold what it cost new: $3,000. I swapped it and some cash for a '59 British nickel-and-dimer sports car so configured that the driver could drop his arm outside and crush a Marlboro on the macadam. Cut so low at the elbow, the car was a magnet for large dogs and often I had to pull away from a stop sign leaning far to my right with some mutt's snout *inside* my ride and snapping at my ass.

The car was in color white, but shortly before I left on my cross-country adventure my father asked me if I wanted to have it painted. My folks had a mom-and-pop auto parts store and as a teen I had to work there. One of my duties, in fact, was mixing paint. It didn't matter that I was color-blind. It was a simple process of having a customer pick out a chip and my following the precise formula to arrive at the right color. Anyway, some grease monkey always owed my dad money and sometimes he had to get it back in trade. Thus the offer to paint my car.

The old man told me to pick out a chip from the book, mix the formula, hand over the keys, and he would do the rest. A single choice from any large field makes me dizzy but

I eventually found what I saw as a pleasant gunmetal gray, unique among the multitude of colors I browsed. In a few days the car was delivered back to K&K Auto Parts. The old man and I stood on the curb inspecting it. Quite a good job to pay off a debt, I thought. My dad looked at it and said, "This is the color you picked out?" I said it was, pleased with myself. He walked away shaking his head. Neilly, the barber, walked by on his way to the shop. He shook his head as well.

"What?" I said.

"Li'l Monk, you got a pink car?"

But, wait, there's more. I requested that on each door the painter tape off my shorthand signature, a **dp** slanted to the left. White on pink.

That's the car I drove across America and around the streets of black LA, I of blond hair and fair skin, looking like a low-rent pimp in training. Since my color-blindness extended to my choice of clothes, my ride and I appeared to belong to each other. Before the riots I was part of the 'hood. I would call on clients, eat at Louisiana Hot Link joints, have my hair cut at black barbershops, drink at black bars, chat up black girls, and no one ever stopped to say, "Who the hell are you?"

On **DUDE** *MAINTENANCE*

Personal maintenance has always been on the top of every woman's to-do list, but dude maintenance is a recent phenomenon. Growing up, I never heard a man utter the hyphenated word "mani-pedi," or either half of it for that matter. Though we did pay close attention to our hair—that D.A. (duck's ass) didn't occur naturally (except in ducks)—once out of our teens we let our hair take care of itself, which for some of us meant bidding good-bye to it. We shampooed our hair with the same soap we used to wash our skin. The word "product" as it referred to hair treatment was not yet in use. Grease was the word. Going gray was proof of maturity. Hard work was exercise enough. Leathery skin was manly. Picture Charles Bronson next to Leonardo DiCaprio. We were Bronson dudes. We were masculine. Toxic now, it appears, but admired back in the day, by men and women alike. (A forty-year-old woman recently cried on my shoulder about her husband: "I just wish he would be a *man*." [Subtext: "Like you."])

Dudes may plan for the future but on a grooming level, we live one day at a time. Which is not to say, live every day as though it were your last. What, like sick in bed and shitting yourself? Live every day like you have a hundred years left, is my advice. Time is a terrible thing to attempt to control. Let it find its own way.

Whenever my mother said, when I was under her roof,

"You either have to get a haircut or take up the violin," I went to Neilly , my Italian barber on South Main Street, and asked for a Pietro Pistole, the simple haircut favored by the manly hero of the *Peter Gunn* TV series, then popular. The Peter Gunn-do appealed to the observer because it was uncomplicated and neat. It appealed to the wearer because it was undemanding. You wet a hand and ran it over your hair from one side to the other. Done.The bonus was that it would be months before your mother would have to repeat her snide remark.

I am blessed with a full head of unruly hair, and since my mother is gone the duty of ordering it trimmed falls to my Exotic Wife. Whenever she says, "I didn't know I was marrying Art Garfunkel," I go to Dylan, a top San Francisco hair stylist who charges $150 a clatter. I am comped, however, because I am his father and I put him through Vidal Sassoon, a training longer and more intense than the police academy, which was his first choice until he got arrested with an animal-rights group for breaking into a UCLA lab and freeing the subjects of their experiments. (I named him after Bob Dylan, whose hair I tried to emulate. Not Art Garfunkel, lady.)

The reason I still have a full mane, apart from having had a grandfather who had one at my age, is that I don't shampoo it unless I have to, and I default to the cheapest shampoo on the shelf because on any given day I can't determine if my hair is normal, oily, or dry, and you have to know that now in order to buy shampoo, or you'll be like the dude who orders a sauvignon blanc with a well-done steak. (Dylan disapproves. He has his own high-end product line and thinks every man ought to pamper his hair with the best money can buy.) Conditioner is a relatively new product, to me. I don't know when it was discovered that hair, like a bicep, has to be conditioned. It's only a way of selling two bottles of stuff instead of one, but I go along with the gag.

I'm grateful for the hair on my head because the once downy hair of my legs is long gone. The once-dark matted hair on my chest, through which the occasional woman liked to run her manicured fingers, is gone as well. The new and unexpected places from which hair now spouts is not where I would like to see it, and in fact I mostly don't: in the ears and up the nose.

Before leaving the house for a social event, my E.W. will tactfully circle me, peek up my nose, stand on tip-toes to peer into my ears, and more often than not will send me back to use a battery-operated contraption invented for the purpose of protecting wives from such embarrassments. She bought me my own illuminated magnifying mirror to encourage me to mow the nasal lawn, but it makes my nose and all the skin around it, meaning my face, look frightful, and I wind up feeling bad about my face. Look away! (See "Chapters That Did Not Make the Cut": "I Feel Bad About My Face (Look Away!)"

Truth be known, I felt bad about my nose long before I started feeling bad about my dick. From childhood I had a deviated septum, which breathing-wise made me feel like I had a cork in my nose. I had the problem surgically corrected as an adult, but that left me with a glass nose. Should I take one on the honker it would wind up flattened against my face, like an old ham 'n' egger. To the average civilized dude a glass nose might not pose much of a problem, but I often seemed to be in close proximity to punches being thrown. A sucker and a sucker punch will eventually find each other. After the surgery, by necessity I became a diplomat. I won't even get into my lost olfactory sense. Odors that might drive others for the industrial-grade mask never seem to bother me, and I never smelt it even though I might have dealt it.

Yes, when my E.W. does her pre-exit examination I feel like a lower life form being groomed by his further evolved mate, but I don't complain. You can always tell if an old dude lives alone, or if his wife no longer cares, by the hair growing out of his ears.

POSTSCRIPT:

On the subject of facial hair, beards are back. They are now required by Major League Baseball, where every player looks like an Amish farmer in uniform. I wear a beard myself some times, from stubble to ten-day growth. I find it good camo for the second chin. (I feel bad about my chin!) (See "Chapters That Did Not Make the Cut.")

Full fuzzy beards, however, are not a good look for dudes, especially the younger ones. Looking like a Montana woods hermit will limit your possibilities in life, unless you have a 100-mph fastball or a .300 batting average. Truth is, most dudes dislike shaving. As a kid, I couldn't wait to shave, and for a few years I enjoyed it as my passport into the fraternity of men. Then it became one more thing I would rather not do. I have enough to do.

Several explanations for why the beard became once more *de rigueur* have been posed, but I believe a contributing factor was the flood of razors on the market. Dudes went dizzy trying to decide which one to use. Forget electric razors, which are useless. I'm talking about what came after that double-edged blade that went into a silver safety razor, and the foams and lotions that came with it. That double-edged blade fit every razor in existence. Now, in addition to a plethora of disposable plastic razors, a staggering array of razors in all colors of the spectrum crowd the shelf, each requiring a specific blade replaced in a unique way. All of these razors are cheap, by the way. It's the blades that are expensive. Don't get me started on pre-shave and after-shave lotions, and the foams, and, God save me, the moisturizers, the one application without which a man turns into a savage, you are made to believe. It's easier to stop shaving altogether.

POST-POSTSCRIPT:

No discussion of unwanted hair is complete without mention of the willful elimination of female pubic hair—the bush, the muff, the carpet, the fur, the copper gate—long an aphrodisiac for red-blooded muff-diving dudes. When did women start feeling bad about the bush? When did they, en masse it seems, decide they wanted to look like ten-year-olds down there?

Ladies, a word. Dudes don't want to see the thing, they want to *find* the thing, to bury their faces in the wild Sargasso and inhale the sea air. About the time women starting shaving down there, men stopped shaving up here. Coincidence?

WHAT *a* RIOT

Though Manzo and I lived within the curfew area, we were ninety blocks, more or less, north of the inciting incident and were unaware of what was happening that Wednesday night. People think the whole thing blew up in one mad moment, but it wasn't that way at all. It started with every black man's abiding fear, a traffic stop by a white cop, and gathered momentum from there. Even on the following day I was unaware of anything more than rumors and warnings. It wasn't until Friday afternoon, while having an after-work drink at a bar on Sunset Boulevard and waiting for a girl to clock out of her job, that I became fully aware of the seriousness of what was happening in my new city. It was hot and bright outside, dark and cool inside the bar. Only three other men were there, one of whom happened to be black. We watched the riot unfold on TV.

The bartender's comment: "They should shoot them all."

My eyes went to the black dude, whose chin slowly and sadly dropped to his chest. The bartender realized what he had said and with mumbles tried to exempt the black customer from his hateful comment, but once the stone is dropped you can't stop the ripples. I finished my drink and left.

I had a date to spend the weekend in Santa Barbara with a legal secretary/flamenco dancer. She had a gig there with her troupe, Something Folklorica, and I had not yet been to

Santa Barbara, which was supposed to be a charming town. I wouldn't know from that first visit because I spent most of the weekend in the motel room watching TV coverage of the riot.

I did catch two of her several performances on the dance floor of a large Mexican restaurant/club. I shouted "Olé!" at the right moments, foolishly tried to execute the unique Mexican cry of great admiration, and drank my first margarita. I learned what a mariachi was. Meanwhile people were being shot down in Watts. I worried about Manzo, my clients, and my colleagues. Though I hadn't been in LA that long, I had a proprietary feeling toward it.

A curfew was ordered. A map of the curfew area filled the TV screen. Where I lived was within it. I could not go back there Sunday morning as planned. I had to stay with the girl at her place in Hollywood, that night and two following nights before the curfew was lifted. I didn't mind. Her place was so much nicer than the room I shared with Manzo. Though a man and a woman may make the same money, or not, the woman will always have a better place to live. It is a mystery, yet obvious in small ways. The pillows, the candles, the light, the cleanliness.

On Wednesday I was able to return to where I worked, one desk among many in multiple rows covering a great expanse of floor. I could return to...let's call it "my building," because for the life of me I can't remember the official name. I want to say Welfare Center but maybe that's only what everybody called it. In any case shortly before lunch someone called in a bomb threat and we had to evacuate the building. We milled about on the street two blocks away, hemmed in by National Guardsmen with hands tight on machine guns mounted to the back of Jeeps. We talked while waiting for the all-clear signal, and all of us, black and white, agreed on one thing: Cops don't know how to talk to black people. This whole riot could have been avoided with three minutes of common courtesy and mutual respect. The chief of police, even after time to reflect on it, described the protestors as "monkeys in the zoo."

Something extraordinary, however, in the area of personal racial relationships started up out there on the street outside the Welfare Center. One of my colleagues, Helene, a girl I fancied from afar, as the Brits always say, slipped a piece of paper into my hand.

"My address and phone number," she said. "If you find yourself trapped in the middle of something try to get to my house. You'll be safe there."

Helene was black as coal and bright as a sunrise, a few years older than I, and far more mature. We worked several desks away from each other and had at times teetered on the curb of flirting, but this was 1965.

Sporadic incidents of violence and vandalism lasted for several days, but eventually things died down to a simmer. Back in the field, in my little pink pimpmobile, I sat down with an elderly client who showed me the entry and exit wounds in his arm. My mother came out to visit a year later. I drove her around Watts. "This doesn't look so bad," she said, comparing the neighborhood to the house and street where we lived when I was a child. "It is, though," I said.

HERE'S LOOKING *at* YOU

As I noted earlier, I am one of the eight to ten percent of dudes who are color-blind. (I am, by the way, a professional painter, so my life in that regard parallels that of an obese contortionist.)

Rosie, my favorite granddaughter, thinks it's hysterical to run up to me and ask the color of her blouse. I say purple or pink or green, guessing at colors that do not exist for me. She falls down laughing. "It's orange!" Another color I often find problematic.

I did not discover I was color-blind until I was seventeen, during an on-campus physical exam upon entering college, which was required in those days. An upperclassman volunteer showed me several cards of circles filled with colored dots and asked me to identify the numbers I saw. I had no idea what he was talking about. All I saw were colored dots. Then he showed me a special card for color-blind people and I saw the number 13, which was unsettling for him because he could not see 13 or any other number.

My handicap went undiscovered for so long because my parents and teachers paid little to no attention to me, which was the way I liked it. When it became my turn, I tried to emulate that method of parenting and teaching. In high school my schoolmates made fun of the combinations I wore and I went along with the gag while failing to see the humor in it. They accused me of being a "nonconformist," an insult in those days. (An equivalent insult was to call someone a "real individual." The Eisenhower years were repressive. [And yet now we find ourselves missing them.]) Thirty-odd years beyond high school, after a long day of bothering trout with fake flies, I walked into a Montana bar wearing a pink fishing shirt and ordered a Manhattan straight-up. The cowboy bartender grumbled, "You got a lot of balls, comin' in here with a pink shirt on." The several cowboys on the other side of the bar fell silent.

I looked down at my shirt and said sincerely, "This is *pink*?"

Once they saw I wasn't a provocateur from the big city (any big city), they slapped their knees and had a Western guffaw at my expense. Like my old schoolmates they saw me as a real individual, but they bought me a beer—the bartender didn't know from Manhattans—because Montanans salute eccentrics.

Most dudes do not want to be associated with the color pink. Nor would I if I knew any better, but to me pink appears as a pleasant gray, sometimes yellow, like the tie I bought on sale yesterday afternoon. Remember the TR-3? Even my dad didn't know I was color-blind, or it's possible he thought I was gay, because I was interested in art and literature and apparently liked the color pink. (How, I wonder, did that square with my always having had a girlfriend, sometimes two at the same time, whose older brothers thought it serious enough to lean on me? [Now as I think of it, every gay dude I know has a girlfriend or two. Even my E.W. during times of bother will say wistfully, "What I need is a gay boyfriend." I never wished for a lesbian girlfriend, though I've had a few, not in the Biblical sense. I don't flatter myself. I once asked a lesbian girlfriend the question posed in the Postscript following Chapter Sixteen. She said, "We don't!"])

In any case, I never considered color-blindness a handicap, even though it did keep me from becoming a fighter pilot. (It wasn't the only thing.) What bugs me more than the the absence of green is how close-set my eyes are. I have to readjust the binoculars after somebody else has used them. I wear sunglasses, even in Seattle, to hide my eyes from the world. Don't look at me!

My eyes started going south when I turned eighteen and began reading like a madman, having avoided reading anything but Archie and Jughead until then. (I had a crush on both Veronica and Betty and spent countless hours finally having to make up my mind, as demanded by The Lovin' Spoonful. I went with Veronica. Brunettes forever!) I read all of Stendhal and Saroyan, the Russian novelists, the Romantic poets, and Milton and Malraux. (I took a semester course devoted to nothing but John Milton, and now all I can remember is *"When I consider how my light is spent…"*, which is enough to keep you pondering for what time you have left.)

First came reading glasses, which were cool because James Dean wore them, too. (More about that later.) Then came all-the-time glasses, and thirty years later the stinking bifocals that have you tripping over your own feet. At age forty came the first "floater," that black dot that you can't stop chasing across your eyeball. Others would follow, and now I can be seen swatting kitchen counters at what I think are ants.

When I hit sixty, or when it gobsmacked me, a miraculous thing occurred: my eyes reversed themselves and I didn't need glasses anymore. I praised the Lord. Sure, I still needed glasses to read, but I could watch a movie, drive a car, and find a giraffe in the clouds without the help of glasses. I was ecstatic. The optometrist warned me, though, that my eyes would eventually flip back again and sure enough they did. The Lord giveth and the Lord taketh away, a trait I find objectionable.

One night I saw little flashes in the corner of my left eye, like some microscopic paparazzi covering a celebrity wedding in Malta. I ignored it for a day or two, which as I said is the dude default solution to all situations. (There is an unspoken protocol: eyes, you can ignore for two days; heart attack, three days; hernia, a month or two; stroke, depends on how bad you're drooling; pneumonia, walk it off.) When a black line appeared across my eye ball and yo-yoed up and down like a limbo pole, I submitted to an examination. Spontaneous detachment of the retina, I was told. Falling-apart syndrome, I figured. It would settle in by itself, the optometrist hoped, then told me not to be surprised if the other one goes as well. It did, that same week. Left behind after the retinas re-nested was a chorus line of fat floaters impossible to ignore, which is why these days I politely decline to read anybody's manuscript.

Optometrist joke: Czechoslovakian dude goes for an eye exam. The optometrist asks him if he can read the bottom line on the chart. The dude leans forward and says, "Read it? I *know* the guy!"

WE'LL NEVER *have* PARIS

Regrets, I've had a few, but only one worth mentioning: I've never lived in Europe. I lived on the Mediterranean aboard a Navy vessel for nine or ten months at a stretch and sojourned in France and Italy for several successive weeks, but never long enough to get a library card.

Once, I had a writing fellowship to L'abbey de Royaumont, a thirteenth-century monastery thirty kilometers north of Paris, where I lived for five weeks like a monk, except for the sex, drugs, and rock 'n' roll. Before that I sublet an apartment on little rue Augereau, just off rue Saint-Dominque. I went there to escape the saturation coverage of the American presidential campaign, the one where the Republican operatives Swift-Boated John Kerry, taking everything that made him exceptional and twisting it to tarnish him: his intelligence, his courage, and his ability to speak French. I thought American politics could not get any worse. (See "Things I Learned for Myself, Sooner or Later.") Another time I was given an apartment across the street from the zoo in Rome, where I was engaged to work on an RAI four-hour television special on the life of Ernest Hemingway. The original script had been written by the director, in Spanish, which was translated into Italian and then into a formal English odd to the ear. I doctored the script, tightening it dramatically in the idiomatic tongue of Hemingway himself, after which it was once again translated into Italian for the producer, and back into Spanish for the director, who agreed it was better now. I never saw the resulting show, but rottentomatoes.com said 100% of the audience liked it, which could mean the two dudes who responded.

To head off any old-age regret, like the one I now have, I cornered my E.W. with a well-thought-out proposal: "Let's move to Paris!" She didn't go yippee so I drew a compelling picture: "We'll live like Parisians!"

Back then I believed that Parisians knew better than we how to live. I still do.

"Too far from the kids," she said.

Wait, what? The *kids*?

Our daughter at that time was forty-two and and our son thirty-seven. I reminded her that our kids were adults with their own kids. I pointed out that they could come visit and have a swell time. I'd show the grandkids Paris underground, the sewer tour, the catacombs, things every child should experience.

"Too far from the kids."

I could not believe a woman, any woman, turning down a year in Paris.

When children leave the nest and set out on their own they feel no guilt over the miles between them and their parents. Why should they? And why should I have to worry about being too far from my children? How far is too far? How close is close enough?

Deflated, I improvised a plan B: "Well, then, how about New York? We can spend a year in New York."

(It was a test. I understand that New York is not Paris.)

Still too far.

Our daughter lived a five-minute walk away, our son all of forty-five minutes by car if traffic was light, but it never is. My E.W. suggested I go live in New York myself and she would come visit. I could take some classes, she said, because I was always taking classes. True that. I need to have homework all the time. I have two degrees, a hunk of postgraduate study, and eight years of community college, where my GPA is 4-point-0. (See again "Things I Found Out for Myself, Sooner or Later. [Part One])

Well, I packed my bag and I did go to New York, on my own. I studied sculpture at the Art Students League on 57th Street and lived in Hell's Kitchen like a New Yorker. I'd heard it said, and now I can agree, that New York is a great place to live, but you wouldn't want to visit.

My kids turned out well thanks to their mothers and their own good sense, cheers, but I don't get parental obligations after the kids grow up. Humans are the only beasts who do that.

When I left home in that TR-3 I let a year pass before I saw my olds again. During that time we exchanged a few letters and I did call them once, from Las Vegas, to introduce them to the girl I just married, that girl who sheltered me from the riot. This was before my E.W., a love long imagined but never expected. If my parents ever squawked that I was too far away it wasn't loud enough for me to hear. For all I know, they were relieved. I never gave it much thought. I was making my own way.

After one of his children did a tragic thing, Marlon Brando, never the Father of Any Year, said something about parenting that I never forgot and often quote. It was to the point, brief, and at the same time both apologetic and explanatory. He said, "I lived my life. They have to live theirs."

POSTSCRIPT:

Upon writing down these thoughts, having worked up a thirst, I went to the reefer for a bottle of iced tea. Consumers of this brand of tea are encouraged to submit six-word memoirs, which can be printed under the bottle cap. Someone wrote, "Wish I could bubble-wrap my son." Pretty sure it was a woman. For sure it wasn't my mom.

Respect.

POST-POSTSCRIPT (Much later):

So Rosie, my favorite granddaughter, has gone off to her freshman year of college, on the other coast of the country. Her mother, father, and grandmother, my E.W., need to know where she is every blessed moment of the day. There's an app for that. Rosie has informed everyone in the family, however, that her location device will be turned off to them. Only one person will have access to her whereabouts. Me! Why? "Because he will not be checking on me every day. Or *ever.* If you really need to know where I am, ask Grandpa."

Respect.

FIVE *things* I DON'T KNOW ABOUT MYSELF

1. If I'm living on borrowed time, who holds my marker?
2. Why do I always want to be where I'm not?
3. Why did I believe her when she said I was gullible?
4. Why am I good in catastrophe but terrible with inconvenience?
5. Why am I indecisive? Or maybe I'm not!

THE MIDDLE of SOMETHING

The streets were uneasy in the aftermath of the Watts riot. Nothing too threatening, more like grief, and an anger over having to fight for dignity with rocks and Molotov cocktails, which in itself is a forsaking of dignity. That atmosphere did not keep me off the streets or stop me from knocking one night on Helene's door. It might have nudged me on. She was taken aback to see me. I mean, she took a step back from the door. Maybe she needed a second to remember I was someone she knew, not some random white dude knocking on her door.

"I'm always trapped in the middle of something," I told her.

"What?"

"You told me to come here if I was caught in the middle of something. You said I'd be safe."

I was nervous, like any other young dude approaching a woman out of his league. Maybe in giving me her address she was only being kind and helpful to a colleague who might find himself in danger. That explanation was as good as any other, but at the time I was not looking for explanations. She invited me into her home.

We had a glass of wine and searched for something to talk about, like why I was there. I parsed the meanings of "trapped," and "middle" and "something" in and out of context, after which she felt the need to tell me she'd been married once. She had a twelve-year-old son who was visiting his father, a man who left her impulsively after only their first real fight. He was out of her life entirely except for the son, an above-average boy whose only deficit was the apparent comfort he felt living in a racist society. She worried about it. Could he not understand what was going on all around him? Could he not realize what the riots were about? He would say things, in that exasperated way kids can, like, "Okay, if it makes you happy, yeah, I'm a victim of racism." She needed him to take to heart her own experience and to see it as a shared heritage, and to be always aware. He was aware, he insisted, and he was fine. Nobody ever called him a bad name or excluded him from anything he wanted in on. If she wanted to feel like a victim, that was her choice.

I didn't know how to respond. I didn't have anything like that. Single into my late twenties, I was childless. I was writing a book, I let her know, a short book but it was taking a long time, and I knew I could not last as a social worker offering applicants excuses instead of help. I couldn't go back to teaching either, even though I was pretty good at it. Trapped in the middle of something. We laughed at how I was beating the hell out of that vague metaphor.

We kissed, and looking back I cherish the natural flow of that moment. Again, it was 1965. Today the racial overtones are all but meaningless. Not so, then. Race aside, though, it's a different risk today, at least for dudes. It's all, Maggie may I? Am I out of bounds here? Is the light green? Should we map this out, draw the boundaries? Back then we didn't worry about all that. We kissed and held each other close and blameless.

"I wonder if you're not just curious," she said.

"Aren't you?"

She nodded and took my hand and led me to her bed. When she came out of the bathroom and toward me her red panties glowed against her black skin, smoldering I could say, like an anthracite fire just below the surface of the earth. Okay, I've gone too far with that, but I have seen exactly that kind of fire and it quickens the blood. Anyway, the panties were soon shed.

I apologized to her, for the stubble on my face. I hadn't shaved. She said, "It feels right." Sharing comfort after the storm, we made a quiet kind of love, and as it worked out, never would again. In days to follow we would often look at each other during the course of our workday and smile secretly.

YOU *don't* KNOW *JACK*

After working in OAA I was transferred to MAA, Medical Aid to the Aged, away from Helene. We would bump into each other and talk occasionally on the phone, but we never saw each other again in the way we had. My new job: when someone who might be over sixty-five was admitted to LA County General Hospital it was my job to go there and interview him to see if he qualified for county aid. This was before Medicare, which would provide some measure of care and dignity to the elderly poor, while mobilizing Republicans to kill the program, a fight that is still current.

LA General is a monolithic facility, the largest health-care provider in the county and one of the largest in the world. One found his way around the place by following colored lines on hallway floors. "Room 1622? Follow the green line." I've already made it a bigger deal out of being color-blind than it deserves to be, but here comes one more example. (It drives me crazy how some comedians will build a whole career out of an accident of birth. "How's everybody feeling? So I'm a lesbian…" I dated a stand-up comic in New York, twice, each date ending with her getting up on the stage of some two-bit comedy club and cheerfully calling out, "How's everybody doing tonight? Everybody feeling good? So I'm Italian and…" She had seventeen jokes about ziti, after which she would remind the six people present of her name and compliment them on being a great audience.)

Inside LA County Hospital I would ask someone to point out the green line and then try to distinguish it from the six other colored lines and follow it to my new client. Sometimes the person would be dead by the time I arrived, which was the second-worst situation; I can't speak for the deceased but it's a yes for me. In that case I became a detective. I would have to go to his last known residence and try to find out if the old dude had any estate, and I mean like change under the sofa cushions. I would have to inventory the client's assets and if they were less than the hospital bill recommend that the county pick up the difference. I would at times have to go to a skid-row hotel, where the deceased's room was already occupied by another unfortunate, and finding nothing left behind be led down into the basement to go through whatever stuff was dumped there in the abandoned-stuff locker. I would look for a business card, a letter, anything on paper that might lead me to his assets, though considering he was on skid row it was unlikely there were any.

It was unpleasant work, but at least I didn't have to talk to the destitute dead dude himself. When I found a live one it was always a painful conversation. The case that finally wrecked me was a wiry little dude who had had a hot-dog stand for thirty years. A hot dog stand in LA was a good investment in those days. Unless you had a heart attack that ate up your savings and then had another one that wheeled away your hot-dog stand. He knew that I represented the charity of LA County upon which he now had to throw himself and whatever pride he had left. He wept as I interviewed him. The whole time. I was a professional and had to hold back my own tears. He didn't want it to end this way. Neither did I. I went back to the office, approved him for aid, and quit. So you can imagine how I feel when smarmy congressmen like Paul Ryan, well-covered by insurance at taxpayers' expense, squawk about the entitlement of Medicare and devote themselves to destroying what passes for a safety net in a country where a middling CEO of an underperforming corporation can pull down fifty million dollars a year for thinking short-term.

I went back to teaching, in an inner-city school where none of the students and not that many of the teachers were white. It was a click or two beyond difficult. The word "challenging" to describe a shit storm had not yet come into vogue. I grew up in a culture of alcohol and was always a robust drinker, but life as a social worker and an inner-city teacher was going to put me in an early grave. I quit to take a position at a wealthy suburban high school. My principal understood. He'd seen many good teachers come and go. He said one had to have a missionary spirit to teach in his school. I admitted to not having that, wish I did. The suburban school was safer and less difficult but with an inverse set of problems resulting from having too much. Given a choice, having too much is better. Having enough is the true sweet spot.

I finished that novel I told Helene about, *The Last Detail*, and it was slated for publication, with some wind behind it. The timing was good. It generated its own climate and was called "The first underground triumph of the '70s." Before publication Columbia Pictures, now Sony, bought the film rights and I quit teaching at the end of the semester.

The producer, Gerald Ayres, invited me to have lunch with some of the people who would be making the movie, including Jack Nicholson, who was on the cusp of becoming a major star. He was recently quoted as saying his role in *The Last Detail* was the best role he ever had.

I had never met a movie star or celebrity of any ilk

before that lunch. The closest I came was shaking hands with Mohammed Ali at a protest rally against the war in Vietnam, and to accomplish that I had to reach over the heads of the people surrounding him as he walked through the crowd. My hand disappeared within his.

Lunch was on the patio at The Source, a spiritual vegetarian joint on the Sunset Strip that was all the rage. I sat next to Nicholson. On my other side was Rupert Crosse, who was to play Jack's partner in the movie. (Rupert Crosse was an engaging actor with a long list of TV credits who had a break-out role in *"The Reivers"* and looked to have a bright future. Unfortunately, he fell victim to cancer shortly before shooting was to begin, and he died at age 45. Otis Young replaced him in the role.) Robert Towne, the screenwriter who would adapt my novel, was there, along with the producer, a couple of other dudes, and a few girls who might have been assistants, girlfriends, or studio executives. Randy Quaid had not yet been cast.

I remember eating the food as a social obligation. I enjoyed the banter about zodiac signs, which were also all the rage then. Jack saw zodiac signs as another way of getting laid.

The lunch lasted two hours. It was fun to see how easily Jack and Rupert played off each other, trading barbs like the characters in my novel. I leaned back in my chair as they talked across me. No one said anything to me and I wondered who at the table even knew I was the author of the book. For my part I can't remember saying a word. Near the end of our lunch, Jack leaned toward me and mumbled something.

"Pardon?" I said.

"Good book," he said.

"Glad you liked it."

Finished with the meal, we all got to our feet. Jack turned to me again and said, "We can talk more about this if you want to."

"Okay," I said.

I saw him again three or four years later, when we bumped into each other at the Golden Globes, where we were both nominated, Jack for *The Last Detail* and me for the script of *Cinderella Liberty*, the third book and first screenplay I wrote since last seeing Jack.

The Exorcist won everything that year. After the awards show as everyone was staggering out into the night I ran into Jack again and said, "Sorry. You'll win the Oscar, though."

As he had done before, he mumbled something.

"Pardon?"

"I'm a lock."

I never saw him again.

I tell this story when people ask me, "What's Jack Nicholson like?"

I *feel* BAD *ABOUT my* PHONE

Caller ID has not thwarted telemarketers, but I assumed it had wiped out the obscene phone call. I can remember a dinner party, before the advent of the cell phone, during which the hostess played on her answering machine an obscene call she received, and the guests tried to identify the voice as someone we might know. Maybe one of *us*. Obscene calls are now archaic. They never made much sense anyway, back when they were common. Whatever satisfaction a caller might have reached from anonymously talking dirty has been replaced by trolling online or some other dark digital pursuit.

I always took for granted that the obscene call was a male offense, like farting. Women never fart. I never heard of a dude getting an obscene phone call until I got one myself. I had just blown out the candle and was drifting off to sleep when my phone rang. Not rang, it doesn't ring. My ringtone is from Laurie Anderson's "O, Superman." *"Hello? This is your mother. Are you there? Are you coming home?"* Anyone around when I get a call freaks out.

I am out of Hard Times, Pennsylvania, from which you escape one level at a time, carrying a temporary visa to anywhere but here, so any late-night telephone call means that someone has died. I answered with a nervous hello, wondering which one of my handful of loved ones had cashed his check.

Without a prelude, a breathy woman's voice announced: "I want to suck your dick."

At this moment, sure, I can think of twenty-six witty things I could have said instead of, "Who is this?"

Said she, "Does it matter?"

(An interesting question. A maxim long accepted by dudes is, "There is no such thing as a bad blow job." Not to argue with that, but I would like to believe, at least within earshot of my E.W., that I am more discerning than others of my gender.)

I make a comfortable living arranging and rearranging words, but all I could muster was, "Well…yeah…kinda…"

"Look, all I want to do is suck your dick and I'm gone."

Sacked for a loss, I rose to the wisdom of Socrates. "Why?"

"I think it would be fun. Don't you?"

This was not the voice of some high-school girl trying to jazz up a waning p.j. party, but that of a mature woman, self-confident and purposeful.

"Is this a random call or do you know me?"

By now my E.W. is on one elbow mouthing silently, "Who is it?" I hold up my free index finger, pleading for time.

Said my caller, again, "Does it matter?"

(Again, an interesting question. Does anything matter? You can post that answer to any question asked of you. Is it raining? What time is it? Does this make me look fat? Red or white? Why was I born?)

"Let's say I've seen you around and thought it would be fun to suck your dick."

Looking off toward Vienna and stroking my beard, I thought, ahh, a manifestation of sublimated desire. The woman does not want to do it so much as she wants to *talk* about wanting to do it.

"Well, why didn't you ask me?" I said.

"That's what I'm doing."

"Face to face."

"I was too shy."

"You don't sound shy."

I had a right to be angry at this intrusion. I had an *obligation* to be angry, to feel violated. Didn't I? A woman would. Why shouldn't I?

The problem is that dudes are not used to physical compliments and are rattled when they hear one. We're told often enough that we are intelligent, successful, skilled, and—not so often—sensitive, but rarely are we told we have a great ass, even when we *do*. At the beach no one says, nice legs, even if we have nice legs. So this little aside: wives and girlfriends, try to say something complimentary about his body. Don't tell him he's a good provider; we are weary of being good providers. Find some part of that sad hulk to adore, if only his fingernails, and maybe he will stop poisoning himself with alcohol and tobacco. I have an idea. Tell him it would be fun for you to suck his dick.

Back to my secret caller. Try as I might, I could not get angry at her, or even feel put out, and given the proximity of my E.W. I could not thank her either. I ended the conversation by archly saying, "Okay, you played your little game, but please don't call this number again."

And, boo-hoo, she hasn't.

I *feel* BAD *ABOUT* RALPH NADER

It's not the sort of thing dudes dwell on, but I've been in more than one conversation when it's been said that, "Maybe everyone is looking for Mr. Right, including dudes." Leading to, "If you were going to turn queer, who would be your Mr. Right?"

In 1975 I was on the phone in the outer office of Sydney Pollack, a top director of the day, known in the business as a prince among knaves. After a day of working with Sydney on a script that was supposed to reunite Robert Redford and Paul Newman (but didn't and never got made at all) I had to make a phone call to tell someone dinner was off. I was sitting and looking at the floor as I usually do while talking on the phone, only landlines in those days, when I sensed somebody standing in front of me. I looked up to see Robert Redford, patiently waiting to talk to me. I went all aflutter.

Now, let it be known that I am a hopeless heterosexual, and like most dudes I fantasize about a woman (for forty-plus years the *same* woman) at least once every seventy-two seconds, but when I first laid eyes upon Robert Redford that day I thought no man should be so handsome. Why not? I was in no position to know the downside of it.

My friend Manzo picked Frank Sinatra as his Mr. Right, hands down, back when Ol' Blue Eyes was still in or near his prime. Dudes of all ages and races crush on Denzel Washington. The final consensus, though, in conversations like this is that Mr. Right should be an undemanding old Jewish dude with a thick portfolio and no heirs. Looking around, I see a lot of beautiful women who came to the same conclusion.

Bro love found me back when Ralph Nader took on General Motors. His appeal to me was, here is a dude who doesn't need *things.* (I've also had an eye for Jerry Brown and the Dalai Lama, for the same reason.) Here was a dude with a best-selling influential book, who single-handedly slew the Corvair and exposed the ugly face of General Motors, who had only one suit and no ride, living in a cheap apartment. My first car was a '47 Chevy—a green I could not see which was repainted blue because a garageman owed my father some money— followed over the years by an El Camino, a Camaro, a Silverado, and a Cadillac Coupe de Ville, so you could say that Ralph rattled some longstanding loyalties.

I was a high-school English teacher at the time and earning eight thousand a year, when I met a young stockbroker at a party. I knew nothing about the stock market and as a child born to parents hammered by the Great Depression I distrusted it. Older colleagues kept telling me that the stock market was the only hedge against inflation and I ought to be putting any extra money into it. I had a folded hundred-dollar bill in my right shoe so I asked the young stockbroker for a tip. He said I couldn't go wrong with General Motors. I bought two shares and had money left over. I followed the progress of my two shares daily for a couple of months, a boring exercise, until I forgot about my position in equities. One evening I watched Ralph eviscerate General Motors on television. I was enamored. I remembered my two shares. I sent them to him with a note saying I was sure he could make better use of them than I could and we should get together for a coffee. He never replied, never thanked me, and I felt hurt. Men are so beastly. Okay, if that's the way he wanted it, he was dead to me.

Though always an activist on issues, I did not pay much attention to individual politicians, who all had the same mother, I thought. When Ralph, however, emerged as a serious fringe candidate for the presidency, I registered with the Green Party and campaigned for him. Like so many other activists at the time, I thought that it didn't matter who was president, if your choice was limited to Republican or Democrat. (I know, I know, but that was before Republicans threw their support behind a psycho narcissist candidate who knew little and didn't want to learn anything more. It wasn't, however, that long after President Nixon was revealed to be a criminal and Vice President Agnew a mobbed-up bagman. Also Republicans. Just saying. So I should have known better.)

Ralph's candidacy reignited my initial attraction to him. I made excuses for his previous behavior. He was a busy and charismatic man. I was but one more suitor in a long line and would have to wait my turn. I campaigned for him and I voted for him, knowing that he could not win. I was under his spell.

I had no regrets until the aftermath of 9/11, when I realized it *did* matter who was President. It mattered a lot, not only to me and my fellow citizens but to the rest of the world. Back then I tried to rationalize my vote as symbolic, since I voted in California where even Republicans are a fringe party. I laid the blame on the Florida Nader voters, but to this day I feel the shame, the regret and the responsibility for George Bush winding up President. I have imagined countless times how better the world would be had Gore been elected President. He did, after all, receive the most votes. That would have happened had the Nader supporters thrown in with Gore. We should have known. Screw you, Nader, we're finished. I never want to see you again. You're dead to me.

Things I FOUND OUT for MYSELF, SOONER OR LATER

(Part Two)

Anything more than a mouthful is more than enough

Divorce is like a wet sack of sand on your back

Don't let them see you cry

A burrito is a well-balanced meal

The basics never go out of style

The best way to keep a secret is not to listen to any

Everybody is happier on roller skates

Never call the cops

Eat it and beat it

You don't have to be loud to enjoy life

Floss

Even sad songs sound happy on the ukulele

All motivational speakers have the same motivation

Chicken sausage is neither sausage nor chicken

Avoid horses

Lou Gehrig did not have Lou Gehrig's Disease

A mental note is only as good as the iPhone it's written in

Don't beat yourself up, it's not a fair fight

There is no such thing as meaningless sex

The lesser of two evils is still better than the greater of two evils

Say no to tofu

Do everything more slowly

Do everything more quietly

I *feel* **BAD** *ABOUT my* **PAD**

(Part One)

A. I live in Seattle. Every March I wish I lived somewhere else, where it's not so damp and you can catch a glimpse of the sun between November and March. In March everyone jumps the gun and drinks coffee wearing shorts and t-shirts at outside tables pretending they're not freezing. I tried living in New York City. It didn't work out. Half the people there were delivering stuff to the other half. I like to do things for myself, and in Seattle that's the norm. If I'm eating restaurant food, I prefer to eat it in a restaurant. If I buy a pair of shoes I like to try them on and acknowledge the dude who offers advice. Whenever it rained in New York, people fought over taxis and acted like getting rained on was the worst thing that could happen to a person at five o'clock in the afternoon. In Seattle you walk and get wet and don't give it too much thought. In New York dudes hawk umbrellas on the street. In Seattle nobody even owns an umbrella. (Though everyone owns three pair of sunglasses. Theories abound, but no answers.)

B. I live in an apartment that I own. Apartment A 6/8, which means that it has two floors, after a fashion. In the elevator you can press a button for the sixth floor or for the eighth floor, but there is no seventh floor, and I'm afraid to ask why. You have to go to the eighth floor to visit my place. You step inside my apartment, hang your coat in the closet, and drop your keys on the little table. That landing is Floor Eight. You walk downstairs to where I spend my time, Floor Six. Metaphysically you've fallen through Floor Seven. My apartment has high ceilings, a working fireplace, and a view of the Public Market and Puget Sound, so I watch the ferries steam back and forth. If I lose a salmon I can walk down the hill and get another one instead of waiting for the original to show up or calling someone to deliver one. The only downside is the doorman, who is annoying. Every time I go outside, he says, "Enjoy!" Enjoy what? And what's it to him? Then if I come back late and a little drunk I feel bad about what he might think.

C. I live on First Avenue. A Korean store which I've never seen closed is next door, and then a bead shop. A beauty salon is on the same side of the street and although they work on men as well as women I've never been inside. Down the hill, as I said, is the famous Public Market, where you can find anything, including some things you wouldn't want to bring back to your apartment. The original Starbucks is there and Asian tourists treat it like a shrine. If you continue down the steps from where they throw king salmons back and forth for the amusement of tourists, you will come upon my saloon, The Alibi Room, where four killer women work the bar and tables, beautiful tough girls, amply inked. The saloon began as a gathering spot for Hollywood emigres but evolved into a quasi-lesbian joint with the ad line: "The Alibi Room: A great place for a girl to meet a girl."

D. I live at my dining-room table, which is also my desk. It has a round glass top thirty-six inches across, and if I happen to be writing whilst naked I can see my dick, about which I feel bad. My desk has no extras. It's just a glass table. My computer is a MacBook. I bootleg wi-fi from one or another of my neighbors, who say it's okay with them. I don't spend much time on the internet anyway. (Like earlier I had to Google Vidal Sassoon to make sure I was spelling it correctly. I wasn't.) I check in daily on one chat room where they have knock-down, drag-out brawls. The combatants don't have to look each other in the eye, which enables virtual fights as opposed to the genuine article. Some dudes see eye contact as a hostile act. "Whaddaya lookin' at?" I keep my glass table neat, because if your surroundings are neat your mind can go ape, but if your desk is in disarray your mind will keep wanting to restore order to your universe.

E. I live in my bedroom. I have only one of them so I try to put it to good use. There is a kitchen, to be sure, with microbrewed beer in the reefer and vodka in the freezer. I used to have a salmon there but it disappeared. I have green tea and shortbread cookies in a cabinet. The kitchen is a pass-through. As I go from the bedroom to my desk, I hang a left and pass through the kitchen. It's a short cut.The bedroom demands more of my time than my desk, my kitchen, my fireplace, or my balcony overlooking Puget Sound. I have about six sleeping disorders, not counting sleep apnea, from jumpy legs and cramps to nonsensical oration, so I need to shut myself up in there for about eleven or twelve hours in order to get seven hours of sleep. If I get lucky I might get a little cardio exercise there, and if I feel good afterwards, I am in love, according to Ernest Hemingway.

POSTSCRIPT:

When Starbucks went public my E.W. said we should buy some stock. "It's a freaking cafe" is what I said. Instead, I invested in a saloon, though Seattle already had as many of those as it had cafes.

I *feel* **BAD** *ABOUT* VIAGRA

As in navigation, hygiene, and firearms, men and women approach sex in far different ways. You've heard it said that the one true sex organ is the brain. You've heard that said by a woman. Would that it were, because the brain does not have to get rock-hard, and that's what sex comes down to in bed, or halfway up the stairs.

Whatever is going on in the brain of a woman, to be a good sexual partner all she has to do is show up. Anything below that makes her a lousy lay. (Because she isn't even there!) Anything above that puts her well on the way to being the girl of your dreams. Dudes, however, not only have to bring to the party a clean and fresh-smelling body and a variety of techniques and a knowledge of the exact location of hard-to-find secret spots and sweet words of love and the right tracks and wine, but also a dick as hard as a mullah's heart.

Men have grown up hearing whispered tales of a legendary substance called "Spanish Fly" which was said to drive women wild. While sailors sought out the stuff in Barcelona (and fortunately never finding it because, though it exists and requires milking an actual fly, it is highly toxic and counts death among its side effects), researchers were trying to discover what could work for men unable—because of age, physical conditions, or the voices in their heads—to hang a washcloth over it. They eventually compounded the right ingredients and called the result Viagra, a game-changer lauded by humiliated men and feared by women who would lose the power to slacken a dick with a titter.

I first became aware of Viagra via television commercials. I scoffed. Pity the poor fool who couldn't get it up without a crank. Years later I had to admit the incidental need of a little boost myself, maybe after a night of being over-served, before finally coming to embrace unashamed the wonders of pharmaceuticals.

Upside, downside. It works, but you have to schedule sex and watch the clock. It takes an hour for the drug to kick in. You don't want to tarry too long, however, because it might wear off before the main event. One solution is to gulp and go but take your sweet time with the foreplay, and doesn't that benefit everyone? Well, yes, except for the woman who was only showing up in the course of things on her "To Do" list.

Remember the "Seinfeld" episode where Elaine was running out of contraceptive sponges and had to decide which partner was "spongeworthy"? Of course you do. We've all seen every episode five times and still crack up. Well, with Viagra now going for seventy-some dollars a clatter, a dude has to decide if this one is worth a tank of California gas. (The answer is yes. You can always take public transportation.)

The good news is that where a problem exists, chemistry finds a solution. Along came Cialis, a daily pill that makes men ready whenever the moment arises, with cautions that include checking with your doctor to make sure your heart is healthy enough for sex. Yeah, right. Find me the dude who wouldn't want to punch that ticket. During a particularly delightful afternoon delight (as you get older you want to have sex earlier in the day), I told my E.W., "Listen, if I should kick it at the height of this, I realize it might be unsettling for you, tragic even, but I want you to know that fate could not have planned it any better, and you should tell the story not with embarrassment but with humor and pride." Her response: "Please stop talking."

(It may be that the one time dudes want to talk is during sex, while that is the only time women do *not* want to talk.)

The greater caution of the TV ads, which are closing in on the saturation point, is that warning about erections lasting over four hours. I've asked around. No dude I know or any dude that they know has ever had a four-hour erection. If only, they say. I can't tell if the warning is based on clinical data or if it is a marketing ploy. In one ad a couple in their fifties are seen painting a bench together, playing tennis, rowing a boat on the lake, all under a smooth voiceover: *"You've always made a great team."* At the end of the ad he gives her that look, the look that says *please, please, please, please, please* and she chuckles as if to say, well, sure, now that you're on Cialis. Then comes the warning: seek immediate medical help for erections lasting four hours. How immediate is it if you've been watching it salute for four hours? And what do they do in the ER to bring it down, show you old Army training films?

I can picture this very couple. Halfway through the third Lionel Richie song and he's still all up in there. She's directed from her back to her knees, to this side, then to that side, to her shoulders, and she starts to feel like a roast on a spit. Twelve minutes in, and she starts to talk dirty, hoping to kick the sprint to the finish line. Now it's fifteen minutes and she fakes an orgasm or two or three. My God, it's twenty minutes so she says, "Darling, I believe I've had enough. Is there anything else we can do?" Like watch *Game of Thrones* on demand?

POSTSCRIPT:

On a related subject: when lesbians have sex how do they know when they've finished?

THE STORY of HALF my LIFE in 214 WORDS

My first existential moment

I'm five years old. My mother is standing on a wobbly chair, hands above her head trying to keep our ceiling from falling down. It is cracking in several places because the coal mines below us are subsiding. She screams for me to go get the neighbor, but I don't move. I know that our neighbor's ceiling is coming down, too. We live in row houses.

Wh*at my elementary school teacher said*

"You there, stop singing."

Wh*at my high school teacher said*

"You there, wake up."

Wh*at my college professor said*

"You have become a Wordsworthian, young man, and thus will be lost to the world of business."

(That news came as a relief. I decided never to work for a profit-making organization. And I never have.)

Wh*at my mother said*

"How can you be a writer? You've never been anywhere."

What I said

"Thanks for the discouragement."

I would not marry

I would never have enough money.

I will be a school teacher forever

I am offered tenure but join the Navy instead.

My life changes

I move to Los Angeles and write a Navy novel. Yahtzee!

TEN things YOU MIGHT NOT KNOW ABOUT ME, NOR CARE

1. I predicted competitive cooking.
(In an unproduced screenplay, "Time in Advance.")

2. The NAACP gave me an Image Award.
(Screenwriter of the Year)

3. School let me start first grade at age five and three months because I couldn't talk. (I could talk but no one could understand me. It was called "tongue-tied.")

4. I was the first to write a novel in which characters called each other "dude." (Other than a western.)

5. One Valentine's Day, Barbra Streisand gave me a boxed pair of underwear. (White with red hearts)

6. I am fond of scrapple but it's hard to find the good stuff. (Some say there is no good stuff.)

7. I attended classes at the University of Havana. (Spanish)

8. Morgan Freeman once prayed for me. (And it worked.)

9. I have passed enough stones to build a wishing well. (Medical science could not explain it.)

10. I once won a bet on a cross-country train trip by doing two hundred and twenty sit-ups in the aisle. (And then excused myself to throw up.)

I *feel* **BAD** *ABOUT my* HAT
(So I Moved to the Desert)

Hats are not for everyone, including maybe me, but I live in Seattle where it rains more days than it doesn't, and it's cold more often than not. If you lived in or around Seattle you would wear a hat, too.

Mine is a Patagonia Polartec Head Sack, inspected by #5, so thank you #5 for your service. Patagonia is a great company. It is good to their employees and was one of the first American manufacturing companies, if not the first, to provide day care for employees' children on the premises. I knew Yvon Chouinard back in the day, in Ventura, when Patagonia was beginning to gain traction. He needed a hundred thousand dollars to get the company over a hump, so five of us who knew and admired him chipped in twenty thousand each and lent him the money, interest-free, in exchange for the employee discount going forward. We all have closets full of Patagonia clothes now because the garments last for decades, after which the company will replace them free of charge. I had three pair of travel briefs for forty years before they lost their profiles. I sent them to a Patagonia repair center in Reno with a note pointing out that after only forty years my drawers sprung. The company replaced them free of charge.

My problem, however, is not the Patagonia part, it's the hat part. My hat, according to Brady T. Brady, looks like a woman's pubis. Ever since he told me that I've felt bad about my hat, which is not to say I have anything against female pubic hair. I adore that. (See "On Dude Maintenance") As I've made clear here, elsewhere, and everywhere, I resent the social movement to eradicate female pubic hair, led I believe by a militant band of Beverly Hills butt-floss wearers determined to defoliate American womanhood down to the last bush, which will probably be found on a lady named Chloe living deep in the north-coast woods of Mendocino. That said, I would not choose to wear a woman's muff on my head.

You might think, if you don't like your hat you can change it. Unless you are me. It was hard enough to choose the hat in question. I don't want to go through that again. Fashion matters because style makes a statement, but what do I want to say with my hat? I don't know. I'm tongue-tied. Certainly not what Brady is saying about it. I could go with the Greek fisherman's hat. You know the one, wool, dark blue or black, flat top, a little piping on the bill.

A hat like that says I'm comfortable with myself. (I wish!) A hat like that is appropriate for my age, a questionable plus. One man's appropriate is another man's boring, and that would be this man. I can't very well go outside wearing a baseball cap backwards, or even correctly, and expect to be taken seriously by anyone, which is the way I'd like to be taken. But the Greek hat, does it look like I'm pretending to be something I'm not? I'm not a fisherman, after all, and I'm not Greek. What's more, I occasionally smoke a cigar, which with that hat would be way over the top. I'm a dude of a certain age who still cares what he looks like, but also needs to keep his head warm and dry.

Now, the Greek hat does come in gray, which might lighten things up a bit. My beard, however, is salt-and-pepper, and it would look like I was trying to match my hat with my beard. The need to match things—belt with shoes, socks with tie, shirts with eyes, that sort of thing—is unmanly and should be avoided.

If I moved to a warm climate I could wear a nice straw hat, something with a wide brim and a hatband of hibiscus flowers. The cigar would be fine, then. I could add rum and get away with it. This tropical dream was just dandy, until I saw myself shaking the hat at swarming mosquitoes. No thanks.

And that is how I came to move to the desert.

What's more, the desert figures in to a long-held dream of mine.

Most people harbor a secret dream of having a small business of their own, and these dreams are different for women and dudes. Women dream of a little restaurant in a nice neighborhood where they can make and serve delicious foods to likable people at reasonable prices, or a quaint bookstore welcoming people who love to read, or a charming antique shop cluttered with treasures left behind by previous generations.

Dudes dream of repairing vintage motorcycles, or in my case, a roadhouse. It should have a jukebox and two pool tables and no drinks requiring more than three ingredients, and no food except pretzels and pickled things in gallon jars, like hardboiled eggs, tripe, carp, or beer sausage sliced lengthwise.

I'd call it The Alibi Room, which is the name of the place I *did* own back in the day but my partners would never allow me on the other side of the bar. I need a bar I can run unimpeded. In my Alibi Room the week would be filled with good fellowship, brass-rail philosophy, and dialogue amusing to the ear. On a Saturday night, to clear the air, a brawl might erupt, but nobody will be seriously hurt and breakage will be kept to a minimum.

Where will you find this oasis? In the middle of the desert, its outer walls sandblasted by summer haboobs. I would live upstairs where I can catch the breeze, with a dark-eyed beauty about whom the mariachis sing achingly mournful songs. (See below.)

For a hundred miles in both directions of a lonely road, I'll erect billboards every twenty miles that say: "SEE THE CREATURE IN THE PIT. THE ALIBI ROOM." Pass that up why don't you.

A must-see attraction. Kids will bug their old man at the wheel, "We want to see the creature in the pit! We want to see the creature in the pit!" Dad will grouse that he is trying to make good time here, but Mom will say what's the rush? Let's see that creature in the pit.

Folks will have to go through the bar to get to the pit in the walled-off back yard and it will cost a little sumpin' sumpin' extra. It will be a deep pit but not so deep that you won't be scared about the creature getting out and eating your brain. I'll need a proper creature, of course. I had an old metaphysics professor who would probably jump at the opportunity, the same one who taught me the Milton course.

If none of that comes to pass, and few dreams do, I'd settle for a nice neighborhood bar. Not your California bar that looks like an ice-cream parlor but a joint where you have to stop inside the door to let your eyes adjust to the dark.

I've lived in so many different neighborhoods and in each my first mission was to find the bar right for me. With one exception. I lived in Marina del Rey for a few months. I might as well have been on the moon.

In my kind of bar unexpected encounters occur with regularity. For example, I once dropped into an old haunt after an absence of several years and ordered a beer. I was riding the Harley back from Sturgis and the once-familiar surroundings were a respite. Before my beer arrived the biker on the next stool turned and tried to focus his red eyes on me. Said he, "I guess you're gonna beat me up, too."

I quoted Robert DeNiro: "You talkin' to me?"

"Yeah, you'll want to beat me up. Well, go ahead, nothin' stoppin' you."

"You're seven feet tall and three feet wide," I said. "I doubt anybody can beat you up."

"That fella did, over there," he said, nodding to a welterweight at the pool table.

"Him and me together might give you a decent workout, but I don't think we could get the job done."

When he accepted that I was not going to fight he leaned toward me confidentially and whispered loud enough to be heard on the interstate, "Ask her to show you her tits."

"Whose tits?"

He leaned back on the stool, a risk in his shape, to reveal a woman in leathers, the missus maybe, who was not that much smaller than he.

"Go ahead," he said, dropping back into a safer position. "She'll show 'em to you."

"I'm good. All respect."

"Ask her to show you her tits," he ordered and this time with the vibe of a threat.

You know how in the movies a silence falls over a room when someone says something not meant to be heard or when an answer holds the possibility of blood? That's what happened. The pool shooters leaned on their cues, waiting to see how I would handle this. Like they'd seen this audition before. Dust hung in the blue-tinged air.

"The lady hasn't asked me to show her my dick," I said. "I'm not going to ask her to show me her tits."

A spray of beer blew out of one dude's mouth and an old lush covered her face and shook with the giggles. A man in Texaco coveralls stumbled off his bar stool. Even the dirtbag biker laughed. "You do this all the time?" he asked.

"What?"

"Go in places and stir up a bunch of shit."

I guess I do. Or did.

POSTSCRIPT:

In 1966 I was alone in Hussong's in old Ensenada, three o'clock in the morning. I was holding down the bar and two Mexicans were at a table. One dude was unconscious, his head on the table, and the other was on the nod, but at their table stood three mariachis in traditional costumes playing and singing their hearts out, lamenting the loss of someone or something my Spanish was not good enough to identify. Even so, I was moved to tequila tears, not so much for the song itself but by the mariachis who were giving us their all. I thought, that's how I want to feel about writing. I want to do it my way the best way I can, even if no one gives an olé, even if everyone is unconscious or on the nod.

MÉNAGE-A-WHAT?

What unholy agreement permits a husband to command a stranger in a bar to ask his wife to display her tits? No one can ever know the dynamics in play in any given marriage. It is hard enough to understand what is going on in your own.

In the annals of activities of adults in the privacy of their own homes it is not uncommon to discover dudes who derive pleasure from watching other dudes have sex with their wives, or wives willing to go along with the gag. If explored within the realm of fantasy, it is hard to find a woman who will deny ever having imagined some other dude assuming the position of her husband in intimate moments. Seldom, if ever, are the cops called. Why would they be? Unless it spills into the realm of reality and one of the participants never got the memo.

Not far from the beach town in which I once lived a trial came on the docket that attracted my attention.

Horace Tarute, 38, a school-bus driver, was charged with rape, though he did not physically participate in the offense. That accusing finger pointed at Phil Burtoni, 24, unemployed. Not so, claimed Phil. He confessed to an act less than wholesome but one that he did not know might be illegal. To wit: slipping into the arms of a warm and willing woman who thought you were someone else.

That woman would be Mrs. Tarute, 32, Horace's wife, who said that any warmth and willingness on her part were the result of vile trickery. After all, she assumed the man who crawled over her was her husband, tardy to bed. Who wouldn't? Imagine her surprise when she saw Horace, her husband, standing by the side of the bed with his hands in the prayer position like an exorcist. Mrs. Tarute, a cashier down to the Safeway, kicked and screamed and bolted out of the bed, both angry and fearful, and ran into the night yelling for help.

I called the Public Defender's Office and identified myself as a journalist, though the only press card I ever had lay yellowing in a drawer somewhere. I asked if someone there might unpack for me this odd chain of events. Someone would try.

Mrs. Tarute's story is that on the night in question she had had a few drinks with her husband at a local bar. He proposed they go home and get it on, before getting any more drunk than they already were.

She awaited her husband in bed but he was so long in joining her that she fell asleep, a common enough occurrence among couples married for more than seven years, which they were. She awoke, she believed, to her husband enjoying his marital bliss. Besides Horace's not making sure she was awake and on board, she felt something else was wrong. Like, he hadn't been gone long enough to grow a beard.

Horace's story was that when he went to join his wife in bed he saw that someone else had pre-empted him. He concluded, as would anyone, that it could only be an intruder, and so he set about throwing the lowlife out of his home. His wife, understandably distracted, he claimed, did not give him a chance to explain.

Consider now, the bearded dude, young Mr. Burtoni. His story was that he was enjoying a few beverages at a public place, minding his own business, discussing casually the issues of the day with the bartender and whoever else cared to join in.

Mr. Tarute, whom he had never seen before, insinuated himself and struck up a private conversation, which is, after all, the second reason people frequent bars. Conversations between dudes often turn to this woman, that woman, and on the night in question it was no different.

I do not know the exact dialogue that took place—I would surely like to—but the upshot of it was that Mr. Tarute invited him to enjoy an evening's carnal pleasure with his wife, at no cost or sacrifice to himself. Mr. Tarute pointed out his wife, engaged in conversation with a woman at the other end of the bar, and Mr. Burtoni found her more than acceptable.

It's a fair question, asked at the hearing: Mrs. Tarute, are you usually such a sound sleeper? Said she: "I believe my husband, my ex-husband, slipped me a mickey."

Young Mr. Burtoni was asked if he did not think Horace's overture a tad strange. "Stranger things have happened," he replied. The experienced prosecutor who had asked the question knew that to be true.

Finally, the same prosecutor asked Horace what kind of man could possible do such a thing. "Exactly!" cried out the feckless husband. "I rest my case."

Tired of:	*Can't get enough of:*
Whoopi Goldberg	Sarah Silverman
Adam Sandler	Andy Samberg
England	France
Champagne	Rosé
Louis C.K.	Dave Chappelle
Bourbon	Rye
Fusion	Meat and potatoes
Kardashians	Obamas
Lobster	Calamari
Leaf Blowers	Rakes and brooms
O.J. Simpson	Robert Durst
Content	Story
CNN	TCM
Kale	Cabbage
Pilates	Thumb wrestling
Shit	Shinola

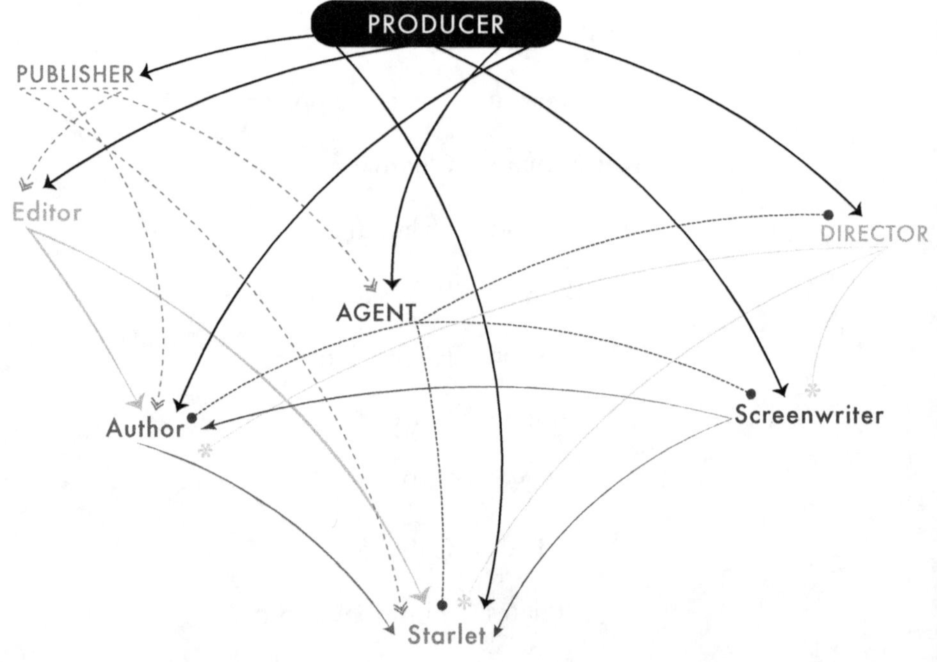
PRODUCER
PUBLISHER
Editor
DIRECTOR
AGENT
Author
Screenwriter
Starlet

WHO *buys* LUNCH?

In the movie and publishing industries, more than simple etiquette determines who picks up the tab for lunch. A tacit protocol exists. I've devised a cheat sheet for rookies.

A PRODUCER PAYS FOR:
Publisher....Editor....Author...Agent...Director...
Screenwriter...Starlet

PUBLISHER
Editor...Author...Agent...Starlet

AGENT
Author...Screenwriter...Director...Starlet

DIRECTOR
Screenwriter...Author...Starlet

EDITOR
Author...Starlet

SCREENWRITER
Author...Starlet

AUTHOR
Starlet

What about an actor? you ask. I have experienced all of the combinations described here, but I can't recall lunching alone with an actor. (The exception would be Paul Newman, and at that time he was assuming the role of producer. He picked up the tab.)

It should be noted that there are occasions, rare, when someone will feel obliged to treat a producer. It's a judgment call. It depends on who wants what from the lunch besides a Cobb salad. It should be noted as well that this protocol is restricted to "above the line" players or whatever they are called in publishing. Costumers and publicity workers can construct their own charts. (It just came into my mind that costumers are called "rag men" and publicity workers are called "flacks," which has me thinking of alternate terms that are used to categorize people who work in the movies, which in turn has me thinking of the struggle to keep up with what people outside of the movies want to be called, because people deserve to be called whatever they want to be called, though it's not always easy to know for sure what that is. Now I will have to do a chapter about that, though I am committed to making this book no longer than Miss Ephron's, which is short. One thing will always lead to another, it is true, but that doesn't mean you have to go there, if you can resist it.)

I *feel* **BAD** *ABOUT my* **MONKEY MIND**

Nobody's got a beef with meditation. Let' s agree it's good for you. It reduces stress. It requires no special clothes or gear, nothing more than a quiet place to sit and fifteen minutes to spare. Some people need the motivation of a guide and the company of a group. Others prefer to go it alone. What all who have ever tried meditation have in common is the realization that it is hard.

I have been meditating for years—for decades—and finally reached enlightenment last Thursday. When we get to how that happened you might say, "Wait a minute, that's not enlightenment." And I will say, "How do you know?"

What's so difficult about sitting, you ask. Awareness of the moment you are in doesn't sound so tough, you say. What's the problem? The problem, for everyone, is monkey mind, what the masters call the mind that will not be still. There is a backward motion in Tai Chi called "repelling monkeys," which recognizes the power of those hairy little beasts to steal your stuff and wreck your day. Monkey mind jumps from branch to vine, swings wildly from here and now to then and there, from when and where to how and why. Oh, wow, it's Mary Ellen, that high-school blonde I swayed with to "Earth Angel," our arms around each other in the smoke-filled dance hall above the bowling alley. How much of the time I have left would I trade for ten minutes more of that? Wonder where she is now and what she looks like.

Don't want to know. Would rather remember.

When monkey mind isn't gliding through steamy jungle air with you tucked under its scratchy arm, it darts underfoot and throws shit in your face, like that time I told a racist joke and fifteen years later realized that it not only wasn't funny, it was deeply insulting to the black family I told it to, who were giving me a *ride*. (Drink played a part.) They were too gracious to call me out. It is a karmic debt I'm still trying to pay off.

Those who have experienced the intrusion of monkey mind in a moment of repose, and that's all of us, will agree that its most frequent demand is, "What's for lunch?" I'll bet even the Dalai Llama had his meditation cushion yanked out from under him by the image of a warm bowl of rice. The only way to avoid that distraction is to meditate after dinner, but in truth it doesn't matter when or where you meditate, your monkey mind will drag you from the sublime you're hoping to get to, back to the mundane you're trying to escape. Simply put, it is unnatural to sit quietly without a thought in your head. Where else can thoughts go?

Failing to sit, I chanted for several years. The chant, which was in Japanese, I think, had no literal meaning to me, but like barbed wire on the range it did fence out the monkey mind. As a result, a fine thing happened. Nothing. Which is the whole idea, or as I like to say, if less is more then nothing is everything. Cool Hand Luke, referring to a poker deal, described it thusly: "Sometimes nothing can be a real cool hand." But then at about the time you think you've nailed it, the monkey escapes and throws shit in your face. Back to cushion one.

In due time I discovered walking meditation and was excited by it, which in itself defeats the purpose. You really don't want to let yourself get worked up about anything. That opens the door to stress. Next you'll be wanting things, which leads to suffering. Walking meditation is exactly what it sounds like, a slow walk to nowhere. You can do it downtown, but it is best done in circles in a bucolic setting, breathing in and out, hands behind the back, measured steps, head down. Oh, look, smooth pebbles. Looks like river rock. That first time I took E.W. fly-fishing in Montana, crazy in love… and she gathered up river rocks…and I had to carry them… and I threw out my lower back…but what the hell, they were free and wouldn't wind up in a kitchen drawer…where *did* they wind up…? Monkey mind.

(Forget all that anthropological posturing about men being hunters and warriors. The human male's true vocation is beast of burden. Dudes have a natural talent for toting stuff, and that's really why women tolerate us, because at any given moment somewhere in the world a woman wants a heavy thing moved from here to over there or transported from a river in Montana to an island in Puget Sound. Even a womanless man cannot walk past another dude securing cargo to the roof of his Ford Explorer without joining in and seeing the task through to completion, to the last bungee cord. "That's not going *anywhere.*")

It is said that there are forty-five thousand ways to meditate, or to live a meditative life. Serving tea…flower arranging…sumi painting…archery…hitting other dudes with poles. Stumbling away from walking meditation, I found Tai Chi. I knew that if I were ever successfully to meditate it would have to involve some kind of movement, and Tai Chi is ethereal fluidity. Tai Chi moves are simple but precise, easy to learn but difficult to execute correctly. To complete a set of Tai Chi requires thinking about nothing else but the position of your feet, your hands, your head, and pretty much the rest of your body, which in advanced Tai Chi floats up and down as your extremities hit their marks, both those marks on the ground and on your imaginary attackers, because Tai Chi, after all, is a martial art. The goal, after years of practice, is to move without any thinking at all, to make it one flowing dance rather than a long series of short moves. Most serious practitioners, myself included, expect to achieve that state midway through the next reincarnation.

I've practiced Tai Chi for fifteen years and still think about what I'm going to have for lunch while lightly stepping through "Four Fairies Work Their Looms." Sometimes I rush it, which is self-defeating because the power and beauty of Tai Chi is in its slow and graceful movements, fast enough only to keep the Chi, or energy, flowing. Free of all other distractions, I'm sometimes derailed by the moves themselves. Why do they call this one "Serving the Tea," when it is clearly a poke in the solar plexus, or why do they called this one "Needle to Sea Bottom," though I don't know what else you would call it, because it is not a defensive move and if it's a blow it's the strangest one I've ever seen.

I will not stop practicing Tai Chi until I am physically unable, but I wonder if that determination is fed by the fear that if I skip even a few days I will forget what follows any given "Single Whip."

A natural cousin of Tai Chi is Qi Gong, which turned out to be remarkable for me. It was during a Qi Gong session that I found enlightenment. Last Thursday.

Qi Gong is best done in a group, in a circle, following an instructor. The moves are as precise as those in Tai Chi and make even less sense. In Qi Gong, the working acronym, according to me, is BAM: breath, awareness, movement. Breathing doesn't count for much in Tai Chi, but in Qi Gong it is dope, and for that you need help. For example, my sensei describes the breathing as "…not in, out, in, out, but inout, inout."

Tai Chi is a set series of 116 moves, done exactly the same way every time. Qi Gong is also a series of moves, with colorful names like "Dragon Washes His Face" or "Pulling Silk," but you don't have to do them in any order. You can mix them up for variety.

Unlike Tai Chi, in which during fifteen minutes you cover some ground—about the area of an unfurnished $3,500-a-month studio apartment in San Francisco—to practice Qi Gong you stand in four square feet for an hour. During each session, you will ask yourself, "What am I doing here?" It's not a workout. It's not standing yoga. It's not stretching, per se. At the end of it, however, you feel much better and believe that life is worth living. It's all about closely communicating with your body, gathering and spreading Qi or Chi, good vibes, energy. The movements are large but the goal is, after many years, maybe lifetimes, to wind up with impeccable awareness and a mind empty as a narcissist's promise while your extravagant gestures shrink smaller and smaller until they are reduced to stillness and silence. Woo-hoo.

But we are not there yet. Though neither Qi Gong nor Tai Chi is sustained meditation under the bodhi tree you are cautioned during each move to tame the monkey mind, through breathing, motion, and stroking your own body, which sounds way more autoerotic than it is.

Anyway, to the session that did it for me. Things were going okay. My stance was solid, my breath steady, my soft gaze passing through the dappled leaves of the tree over the sensei, except for glances at one old lady in the circle. Qi Gong is not a competitive sport, and no one is going to hit you with a bamboo stick if your moves are not exquisite, but this lady's moves were outlandishly wrong. Instead of gently rocking her Qi ball, an imaginary space between your two open palms, she was waving her hands in the air like she just didn't care. She was in her own world. I thought, maybe she really is in an alternate world imposed on her by the ravages of time. As in, senile. What caught my attention as well—and I believe the old gal was the only one getting this part of it right—was that in the opening inventory of "checking in," of feeling the earth below your feet, etc., you are supposed to lift the corners of your mouth in a gentle smile. The old lady had that down. I'm calling her an old lady but she may not be any older than I. She may be *younger.* She was enjoying herself, smiling away. How far was I from senility? When I arrived would I be smiling, or screaming, "There's bugs in my hair!"

Nearby, two leaf blowers were having at it, an obstacle to gathering any decent Qi. (Those of you who have read *Eternal Sojourners* will find this familiar.) The leaf blowers sounded like amplified dentist's drills. You know they will stop but you don't know when. The problem is they have triggers. *"Pry my cold dead fingers…"* I watched the leaf blowers through "Fisherman Casts His Net," and saw that, all by themselves, they were a theatre of the absurd, two high-powered dust bazookas chasing six leaves over half an acre. They took me out of the moment, to be sure, and I slid into wondering if spreading Qi has an application to sex. I should add something about that to the chapter on porn, I thought.

The night before, I watched Bryan Cranston's performance in *All The Way* as LBJ. Transformed himself. He's in my last movie. Not LBJ. Bryan Cranston. Inspired casting.

Cranston would not remind anyone of the original Billy Bad-Ass. Good actor. *Breaking Bad* was as good as anything I've ever seen on TV. I didn't watch the whole LBJ thing because I was gagging already on politics. It must suck to be Paul Ryan. I'll bet the devil never even gave him a receipt. The real order of his priorities: political future, my party, then maybe my country. Can't be happy. When I do "Gazing at the Moon" my shoulder hurts. Maybe I should see Doctor Z. How come all my doctors are women now? I should write something about that. Everyone in cable news? Big karmic debt. Would my father do this, Qi Gong? No way. He wouldn't do Tai Chi either. I should do a list of things I do that my father would never do. It could be part of the book. Lists of questionable value. Of dubious concern. Of impertinence. Of startling pertinence, actually.

See what I did there?

While I was "Boxing The Tiger's Ears," my monkey mind would not, could not, lay off kicking my ass. I chastised myself, for the one hundred thousandth time, and that's when it happened: Wait a minute. Why have I been fighting monkey mind most of my life? What's stopping me from admitting it: *J'ai un esprit de singe, donc je suis!* (I have the mind of a monkey, therefore I am.) I haven't been doing all this—meditation, chanting, walking, Tai Chi, Qi Gong—to lock out my monkey mind, I've been doing it to uncage the little bugger!

Most of this book, I discovered in the moment of my epiphany, was shit thrown at me whilst I was trying to find inner peace somewhere else. When this wins the National Book Award I'm going to have to thank monkey mind publicly and let them sort it out.

What you can't keep out, invite in. Enlightenment!

I *feel* FUNNY *TELLING* COLORED GIRLS *my* NAME *is* DARRYL

(Part One)

Off the coast of Cuba at 19-45 North latitude, 74-45 West longitude, is Point Daryl. I was up on the bridge standing a mid-watch, and the officer of the watch was charting our various locations. All of those sites needed a name so he asked me, "You want a point named after you?" Sure, who wouldn't? "What's your first name?" I told him. He misspelled it, which is the curse of my life. One of them. I have three names, each of which is misspelled one hundred percent of the time.

My mother, who was a big movie fan, wanted to see *International Settlement,* the new 20th Century Fox release, but she was in an advanced state of pregnancy (with me) and wasn't sure she could handle the intensity of murky arms dealing in Shanghai and everything like that. She asked my father to take her, an outlandish overture.

I never knew if my father didn't like movies generally or if he felt they were not worth the time he could have spent playing poker at the Elks.The only time he ever went to a movie was when he was dragged there by my mother, like this time, or later to movies I wrote.

I would be their second child. Their deal was that Mom would name the first one and Pop would name the next one. (The last one as it turned out, by choice or surrender I never knew.) She chose Ronald George for my brother, RIP, a reasonable name for a baby who grew to be a reasonable man, called Ronnie by everyone. I'm guessing he was named after Ronald Colman and George Raft. What luck. And then the following happened while I was enjoying my time in the womb, waiting to enter center stage.

The house lights at the Capitol went down and the curtain was drawn. (Movie theaters really did have curtains in those days.) Fade in. My life, before I had a chance to try it on, was already burdened by a family name no one could pronounce or spell, and in that moment, thanks to Dad, it would be complicated further.

The movie was *"Produced by Darryl F. Zanuck and Sol M. Wurtzel."* My father whispered into my mother's ear, "I like that name." "Which one?" she asked. "Darryl," he said. He had never seen nor heard the name before but now he knew he wanted a son named Darryl, or a daughter by the same name because it looked like it could cover either sex. (Had my opinion been asked, I would have gone with Sol.)

The reason my dad liked the name is the same reason I didn't. All through school, including college, I never met another person named Darryl.

My father's name was Frank. I would have been happy with that, though I would not have liked the Junior part.

Much later I learned that had he not jumped at the first name he saw on the screen he would have had a wider selection in the acting credits. I could have been Keye Luke, splendid, or, wow, Pedro. I would loved to have to have been named Pedro. (The actor's full name was Pedro de Cordoba! Who couldn't get laid with a name like that?)

Pop could have named me after his father, John, which would have been fine, but nooooo. To make matters worse, for my middle name he gave me the masculine version of his mother's name, Gizella. It took me twenty-five years to run into another Darryl, but I have yet to meet another Gizell, and I've been around a long time. (Naturally in elementary school I was called Gizmo.)

Once I asked my mother how she could stand by and let an innocent child be saddled with a name like that, considering our unusual family name. (Americans, I have concluded, find it impossible to write a "c" before an "s" unless they live in Tucson. With the exception of the Arizona city, every time they see a "c" before an "s" they feel obliged to pronounce it, even though it sounds strange. If I write my name on a piece of paper and ask you to copy it, you will put the "c" after the "s." You won't be able to help yourself. Those of you, again, who read *Eternal Sojourners* will be aware of this.) My mother replied: "A deal is a deal."

I was in the Navy before ever meeting another dude named Darryl. In the pre-dawn chow line at boot camp, Great Lakes, Illinois, dead of winter, freezing our asses off, I heard some dudes behind me talking and one of them said Darryl something. I spun around. What? Four black dudes. I asked which one was Darryl and then told him that I was Darryl, too, and he was the first dude I ever met with that name. They acted like I was a culture appropriator. Black Darryl introduced me to one of the other dudes, who was also named Darryl, only he spelled it Darrell. Darryl and Darrell were homies and said they knew other dudes back in Detroit named Daryl or Daryle.

Years later I knew them too. They all grew up to be Darryl Strawberry, Darrell Green, Darryl Dawkins, Darrell Griffith, Darrell Armstrong, Darrell Jackson, Darrell Arthur, and hundreds more. All black dudes.

As a result, and I'm sure you've noticed this, whenever a TV script writer has to come up with a name for a black character he goes for Darryl, the new LeRoy. If you use the name for a white character it becomes inherently funny, and on television whatever is funny is doubled down. Thus, "This is my brother Darryl, and this is my other brother Darryl."

What follows are just some of the spellings—from my point of view, misspellings—of the name Darryl:

Darel	Darryline
Darille	Darryll
Darolyn	Darrylyn
Darrel	Darrylynn
Darrell	Darylene
Derrell	Darylin
Darrelle	Daryline
Darrellyn	Daryll
Darrill	Darylynn
Darrille	Daryl
Darrylene	Darylyne
Darrylin	Derrill

Note that the name is feminine as well as masculine, so it's not only the new LeRoy, it's the new Leslie.

WHY *it is* CALLED *A WAITING ROOM*

Buddhism has laid out an eight-fold path to end suffering, all involving the "right" thing to do. Number Five, for example, is "Right livelihood." It's not rocket science; it's easy to identify the wrong livelihood. (And yet "Rocket Scientist" may well be a wrong livelihood. The fundamental Buddhist committed to enlightenment sees only begging as the right livelihood, possessing only what sustains life, but that may be too much for you to understand, and when I say you I mean me.) I'm going to go out on a limb and say healing is a right livelihood.

I have a few doctors among my personal friends, and I admire their skills and dedication. What I don't like about other certain doctors is their inflated sense of their own importance, bordering on arrogance. What used to be bedside manner has become intimidation. We no longer revere our doctors, we fear them. We fear their organization, the AMA, as we might any other special-interest group. They are not exactly thrilled with us either. Each of us is a potential lawsuit or an unfair attack on Yelp.

I entertained these notions once while boring myself silly in a doctor's waiting room. Nothing wrong, thank you, I was there at the behest of an insurance company that wanted a read on what kind of mileage my body had left on it. Although life can end abruptly, one's obligations go on, and certain people have to protect their interests.

Who enjoys physical examinations? The room is too cold;

the light gives a blue tinge to your skin. The probe he sticks into your ears reminds you of an initiation rite into a fraternity you didn't want to pledge anyway. And then there is that dreaded moment when the doctor tells you to turn your head and cough while he tries to lift you off the floor with two fingers, and that equally dreaded moment when he tells you to hike up your gown and bend over.

I arrived fifteen minutes early, as requested. Obligations are obligations. I thrive on them. The more I have the better I function. I was given a clipboard and several sheets of questions to answer. I'm suspicious that no one reads those things anyway. I looked for a seat in the crowded waiting room that was not within coughing distance of someone who might actually be sick with something catchy.

No one talked. We sat glumly as though we were in a holy place when we'd rather be at the movies. During the next twenty minutes no one entered or exited the inner sanctum. It occurred to me that never in my life has a doctor seen me at the appointed time. I've accepted that because doctors are important professionals and their schedules are subject to change. I'm not entirely unimportant, but if I have a change of schedule and miss my appointment I still have to pay.

Another twenty minutes passed. I had an insight into why we are called "patients." Someone finally grumbled and said he'd been waiting for over an hour. Neither doctor, nurse, nor receptionist offered any explanation, he said.

Since I was not in need of medical attention, I left my seat and walked out of the office. I calculated that my time was as valuable as the doctor's, so when I got home I invoiced him for the missed appointment. He did not remit. After thirty days I added an interest charge and after another thirty days I sent it off to a collection agency. They were amused.

FIFTEEN THINGS *I DO* THAT *MY FATHER* WOULDN'T

1. Qi Gong
2. Tai Chi
3. Read poetry
4. Go to movies my son didn't write
5. Drink fine wine
6. Vote Democrat
7. Have a serious talk with my son
8. Eat sushi
9. Baby talk to a dog
10. Barbecue
11. Play the ukulele
12. Sing
13. Fly first class
14. Wear jeans
15. Live in California

FIFTEEN *THINGS my* FATHER DID THAT I *WOULDN'T*

1. Play poker at the Elks

2. Join the Elks

3. Drink a beer with a raw egg in it

4. Vote Republican

5. Eat pigs' feet in jelly

6. Join the Masons

7. Attend church

8. Join the Eagles

9. Read *True Detective* magazine

10. Be a Scoutmaster

11. Listen to baseball games on the radio

12. Join the Rescue, Hook, and Ladder Volunteer Fire Co.

13. Wear suspenders

14. Go to a barber for a mustache trim

15. Live in Scranton

ALL my DOCTORS are WOMEN NOW

I never thought about it when she was alive, but for her whole life my mother had to have men attend to all her medical problems, which fortunately were few. (She died at eighty-eight, essentially drying up and drifting away.) This had to have been an ordeal because a woman doesn't want a male doctor touching or looking at some things. In those days women had no choice.

Dudes, as well, are not crazy about having their junk inspected by hospital nurses, but in terms of ongoing medical care we have always been able to find a doctor of our own gender. (When did "the family jewels" become "junk"?)

When my primary-care doctor decided to specialize in diseases of the rich, my E.W. suggested I try her doctor, Dr. Kathy. To my credit as a dude of a different time, I never gave it a second thought. Until midway through my new-patient physical examination. After a discussion of my medical history and the taking of my vital signs I remembered what always came next. The last thing. That thing. The finger wave.

Dudes tend to be too graphic when describing medical procedures, so I'll make this brief. Over many annual physical exams and a variety of latex-covered middle fingers I grew used to the prostatic assault. Bend over, elbows on the table, hold your breath. Up goes that wiggling finger and digs around in there like it lost its wedding ring.

Dr. Kathy, on the other digit, asked me to relax and lie on my side, facing away from her.

"A little enlarged," she said, "but nothing to worry about."

I heard her strip off the glove.

"You're done?" I said.

I hardly felt it! Never take a woman's touch lightly. (It's a beautiful thing.)

She would still be my doctor if I hadn't moved to another city, where I found another doctor who also happened to be a woman, and when I moved to still another city I found still another woman doctor. Not that I sought them out. It just worked out that way.

But before all that moving around, one day I was reading a paper and the print started bouncing. I looked up and saw that the whole room was bouncing. It lasted for only thirty seconds, but it felt like the first half-minute of the last of my life. I called a friend, a retired neurosurgeon, who told me I ought to go see his neurologist. (This friend once had to have serious spinal surgery himself. He knew how serious it was because he had performed the operation numerous times. The day before his surgery he told me he hoped that when he came to he wouldn't be on a respirator because if he was he would have to stay on it. For his own operation he selected the best neurosurgeon in the city, Dr. Kim, a young Asian lady. The surgery was a success, by the way.)

Dr. Kim ordered an MRI for me, suspecting a mild stroke. (There are such things, mild strokes, but only when they happen to someone else.) The results were unremarkable. My episode fell under the category of "Just One of Those Things." (I have a history in this category of disease. My heart, for example, was bopping between 40 and 190 beats per minute. I spent a working week having five different tests and another week wearing a heart monitor. At the end of it, the cardiologist, an Asian kid of around twenty, told me all the tests were normal. I said, "But what about the symptoms? They weren't normal." She said, "No, but normal for you." Just one of those things.)

In the new town to which I migrated, I read about a family of dentists: father, two sons, daughter, and daughter-in-law. Every one of them a dentist. You can only imagine what dinner must be like in that family. I opted for the daughter, Dr. Sherri, believing, correctly, that she had always had to try harder. In the same town I was recommended to an O.D., which is a doctor who flunked Latin. Dr. Lily was a Filipino lady who never spoke above a whisper and who would diagnose me in the parking lot if I didn't have an appointment. For a MOR surgery on a basal cell carcinoma, Dr. Marie, a surgeon, whittled away at me five separate times during the course of the day, wearing what looked like a Plexiglas welder's mask. My anesthesiologist on another surgery: Dr. Abby. In Palm Springs, I have Dr. Z. (I can't pronounce her name. She's Indian-American. She can't pronounce mine either.) Instead of whisking me in and out, like dude doctors used to do, she takes so long sorting out all the aspects of my various conditions that I sometimes ease inconspicuously to my feet and inch toward the door, like a plus-one at a party he didn't want to attend. She says I'm "complicated." Medically speaking, no one wants to be special.

I have two acupuncturists, Dr. Su, who is Chinese, and Dr. Helga, who is German, and who is the only person ever to recognize that the tattoo on my back shoulder is a Picasso sketch. Whenever I see Dr. Su, every Monday, she says, in a soft voice that kills me, "Did you get out last weekend? Did you spend some time with friends?" She is attempting to cure what she believes may be an allergy to other people, but finding the right meridian to pin that is proving challenging.

This may seem like I'm trying to curry favor with women, who are likely to be the primary gender buying this book—because women are the primary gender buying all books—but the truth is I myself am mystified. Twenty years ago all my doctors were white Anglo men. Now, with the notable exception of Dr. Dark, my urologist, all my doctors are ethnic women, not to mention—though it looks like I'm going to anyway—my lawyer, my accountant, my agent, my tarot-card reader, and my alter ego, Anne Argula, who wrote my mystery novels.

So, as my E.W. likes to say, there.

I *feel* BAD *ABOUT* PORN

(For the most part)

It is likely that I am not now, nor have I ever been, the voice of my generation. I don't know who is, nor why. I am not even sure to which generation I belong. I was too late for The Lost and The Greatest, too early for The Boomers and all that followed. The timing was right for The Beats and I may have flirted with it for a year in college because the poetry was more appealing than Milton, though not as enduring. In the end I could not handle a life of dingy T-shirts and sandals. On the subject of porn it is possible that I do not speak for all men. Or for *any* men, other than myself.

The first porn film I ever saw was *Deep Throat*, which at the time was all the rage in Los Angeles. It played to full houses at a legitimate revival theater and was lauded by mainstream above-the-line Hollywood players as breaking new ground. The new ground it broke was the appearance of Linda Lovelace, who could take into her mouth the entire length and breath of any dick presented to her, no matter how large. Her technique, though impressive in this application, had long been employed by sideshow sword swallowers and was soon learned and practiced by other porn stars and promising amateurs. In short time the broken ground was already raked over. It was much like what happened when Michael Jackson first did the Moonwalk on stage and blew everybody's mind. A week later fourteen-year-old kids were doing it at birthday parties.

The enthusiasm for *Deep Throat* from major film directors cleared the way for others to admit without shame that they enjoyed pornography, too. On the recommendation of an A-list director with whom I was working at the time, I went to see *Deep Throat*, with his secretary as my date. The director looked forward to talking about it the next day. After the initial shock of watching a huge dick disappear into Linda's face, we sat dumbfounded through the rest of the short film and had nothing much to say at the end of it, beyond "Well, that was something."

All these years later, what I remember most about *Deep Throat* is the short "documentary" before the main feature. Its conceit was that it was being shown as an instructional movie for married couples, and it did have that Eisenhower-era vibe. An attractive couple demonstrated, with a step-by-step voiceover performed by, let's say, a sexual therapist off-screen—because most sexual therapists look like someone you would not enjoy having sex with—what they considered a pleasant night at home after the kids were tucked into bed. I enjoyed it. The couple were attractive, normally endowed, and seemed to care for each other. For all I knew, they were married. The sexual techniques they shared with the audience were gentle, slow, and pleasantly familiar. My kind of porn, I discovered.

(An aside: a year after the success of *Deep Throat*, I met Linda Lovelace. This encounter, told here in its entirety, occurred at the Playboy Mansion, during one of "Hef's" famous Sunday-night parties. I was a last-minute plus-one with a producer who was a regular there, and, after submitting to some overreaching security screening, I was permitted inside. I was introduced to the Playboy himself, who was in pajamas and a robe drinking a Pepsi. I thanked him for if not inviting me at least for allowing me inside. I was introduced as a novelist/screenwriter working on a project entitled *Tom Mix Died For Your Sins.* Hefner said, "It might as well have been him."

I met the regulars that night, Bill Cosby among them. I talked to Cosby for three minutes, long enough to discover that he was, sadly, an asshole. I found Linda Lovelace standing alone in a small game room lined with pinball machines. She stared down at one of them but did not play, as though it were an object of mystery. She appeared forlorn, so I went to her and said hi. I did not say I was a fan, which I wasn't, nor did I make any reference to her claim to fame. I told her that I was a pinball wizard as a kid but grew out of it. [Don't read too much into that.] She asked me to demonstrate, which I did. Linda was impressed in a spacey sort of way. She seemed to enjoy the dings, the dongs, the lights flashing on and off, the flippers batting the steel balls.)

After *Deep Throat,* no more porn crossed my path until I came into possession of a VCR recorder. An actor friend of mine, famous as one of the Tarzans, when told I had bought and hooked up a VCR player, gave me a cassette, a porn reimagining of Catholic schoolgirls in their uniforms having a fun time. The accepted reality of Catholic schoolgirls is charming enough. I found the tape disturbing.

Then came the internet and YouPorn.com, which I read about in *Esquire,* and of course followed the link. The sheer volume of international porn on this single website is overwhelming. The insult of these offerings, unlike Deep Throat, is the complete disregard for any story, production values, or humor, which I believe must be an essential element of porn. (An essential element of everything, really.) The hook is that this stuff is all done by amateurs, girls who love to do it for the birdy and are up for whatever humiliation is thrown their way.

Thumbnail stills describe the library and each is rated on a percentage basis by previous viewers, so you don't have to waste your time on stuff that nobody liked.

The only videos I can endorse are in the girl-on-girl genre. The only true positive test of heterosexuality, by the way, is that a dude is turned on by two or more women going at it. That's science. But why is that? Maybe because women are nicer to each other, even in porn.

On a higher level, a Zen level, sex is energy. (What isn't?) If you go too slow you stall the Qi. Go too fast and the Qi evaporates. Porn simply gets it all wrong—one ought to see sex as slow going but present and aware, until transcendence becomes inevitable. Otherwise, porn sucks.

I feel BAD ABOUT THE ODDS

I was never driven to have things you can hold or look at. It's been that way since childhood. That's a fine quality to have when you're poor and it's helpful even when you're rich. I've enjoyed the things I've owned but I've not waged war to attain them and I don't go nuts when I lose them. Sometimes I've enjoyed and hated my things at the same time. (See "I Feel Bad About My Murse.")

Both my parents died with practically no possessions, no large assets like a house or a car or jewelry; and the few things they did leave behind, clothes and furniture, went right to thrift shops. Unlike them, I do have three small collections, mainly because somebody started me out by giving me the first of something I found pleasurable enough to fill in with a second or third. Fountain pens, knives, ukuleles. That's it.

Like most young men of my generation I wanted a car, and had one during my senior year of high school. When I went off to college I sold it and felt relieved of the burden. I had a boat a few times and like all boat owners who don't earn their living on one I was glad to be rid of it. I wear no jewelry that isn't utilitarian or sentimental. I have hardly any interest in clothes. People are mildly insulted to learn that I don't even care where I live. The town, of course, is important but the house itself doesn't matter, as long as it is warm and dry. (Once again, if you've read Eternal Sojourners, you already know this. It's key.)

Old age comes with few advantages, but for me one of them is that I find there isn't a thing I want. I'm a problem to my family come Christmas and my birthday. They wind up giving me a pen or a knife or a ukulele.

So why do I play the lottery every Tuesday and Friday afternoon and spend the evening planning how I will spend the money?

I don't enjoy gambling, though I go to Reno a few times a year. (I go for the food and the art, don't laugh.) Sitting for hours at a blackjack table or a slot machine is not much fun, win or lose. I currently live in a city with a casino but I never go there.

It's the long shot—the really long, long shot—that I enjoy. True gamblers call the lottery a sucker's game, and they are right. But the odds against you are only 303 million to one, so technically you do have a chance. I usually buy my ticket at the same place and each time I do I tell Kathy the bartender, "I probably won't win." She does not disagree, but here is the thing: eventually someone does win. Eventually someone *has* to win. Why not me?

The longer it takes for the winning numbers to come up, the higher the prize rises, until even seasoned gamblers, frugal grandpas, and celibate priests will risk five dollars against the impossible odds of winning five hundred million dollars.

Should I win I hope I'm not the only one, because half a billion dollars is too much for any one person to add to his bank account overnight. But let's say that part goes against me and I wind up being the sole winner of twice the amount of Mitt Romney's fortune. What then?

Federal and California income taxes will relieve me immediately of a good hunk of that fortune. Ballpark, let's say I'm left with three hundred million. Am I disgruntled? I don't think so. If I invest the money at five percent, a threshold that even a blind Chihuahua can reach, I will have an income of fifteen million a year. And after they tax that I will still have eight or nine million to spend any way I want, and if I know only one thing about myself it is that I could never spend that much money every year. Or during any year.

Though it isn't a hard-and-fast rule, everyone who wins the lottery buys a Mercedes. The car I have now is a 2012 Nissan Juke. It has all of 20,000 miles on it and it does everything a car is supposed to do, except impress anyone who walks by it. If you've ever seen a Juke you would not be surprised to learn that everyone who doesn't own one hates it. I could buy a bigger house, but the one I live in now has a room or two I never go into and it's walking distance to town. I might have to move anyway, to some town where no one knows I have three hundred million dollars.

I could give the money to my kids and tell them they don't have to work anymore, but I worry what they would do instead. I could set up trust funds for my grandkids but how do I know that money won't land in the robed lap of some cult leader?

Am I'm forgetting something?

California is a community-property state. Though I may have bought the winning ticket my E.W. gets half the loot. She does not have my aversion to things and might have something to say about putting a dent in our newfound fortune. All marital discord revolves around matters of sex, money, or the kids, so a windfall of these proportions is bound to rain some piss on my marital bliss. The odds of finding an umbrella for that, however, are reasonably good. It's only money.

HELP ME RHONDA

It annoys me when *Variety* and *The Hollywood Reporter* refer to screenwriters as "scribes." The trade papers call directors "helmers," which is to say the captains of great vessels. They call actors "stars," glittering bodies in the firmament. But for writers they conjure up the image of a pale hunched-over weakling wearing a visor and taking dictation. That language spells out a pecking order that has no place in reality. Without writers the visions of directors cannot rise above their martini glasses, and the performances of actors cannot go beyond their own full-length mirrors. I already mentioned the practice of calling costumers "ragmen" and public relations reps "flacks." Likewise, condescending. Someone is called the "best boy" but nobody knows what he does or even if he is a boy. He could be a girl. Every industry has its own arcane ways of identifying people by what they do. You can complain but it will do you no good.

More important for the outsider is to know what to call an individual who happens to be part of a group by virtue of his birth. If there is a consensus in the group, then those of us not in that group ought to call people who are in the group by the name they prefer, if someone can make it clear what that is. People make honest mistakes, but it must be made clear what is derogatory, what is plain wrong, so that those who knowingly use derogatory language can be shunned by the rest of us.

Did you know, for example, that "dwarf" is acceptable but "midget" is not? Do you know why? Neither do I. Most people in this group, I understand, prefer "little people" and ask that the M-word be avoided. The problem arises, in my experience, when trying to describe one person to another person. I can say, "She works in HR, long blond hair, computer whiz, a little person." "How little?" "You know, little." I would never describe anyone as a dwarf, because I don't really know what that means. I think a dwarf has anatomical features that not all little people have, and then there is the unfortunate reference to creatures of folklore.

It's fair to describe someone as a homosexual, but not a queer. The word "queer," though, is common within the group: "We're queer, we're here, get used to it." And just last week it seems "Q" took its official place at the end of the line in the descriptive alphabet whip, LBGTQ. Queer is a word one may call himself but if you are not part of the group you must not use it. That said, I see "queer" being used in mainstream journalism as a context for certain women's groups. Back in 1955, however, when my generation was busy inventing rock 'n' roll, homosexuals objected to the word queer, as well they might since the word always meant odd to freakish.

So the Committee on Nomenclature unanimously voted to adopt the adjective "gay" to apply to all homosexual men, and why wouldn't they, since the word conjured up happy people skipping off to some amusing activity. (Gay would later describe women as well, though the ladies prefer "lesbian" and I don't blame them, since that word has a reference to an exotic island seldom visited but once seen rather enjoyed.) The historical pathway to "gay" took a switchback in the nineteenth century. Back then, "gay" was used to identify a prostitute, as well as the men who patronized her. Go figure. Whore houses were known as Gay Houses. (Note to self: What do prostitutes themselves prefer to be called? Whore, hooker, call girl, escort, VIP concierge, entertainer, sex worker, or prostitute?)

Though also used as a noun now, sexually speaking, the adjective "gay" was once a verb, as in "gay it" which meant having sex with a prostitute. The term evolved by the 1930s to describe a man who had sex with other men, and in 1955 it became official because "homosexual" sounded far too clinical, as if it were a disease, which indeed many people of the time believed it was. (Many people still do, including some gays, but these are generally the same people who believe President Obama is a Muslim born somewhere in Africa and that Trump has their best interests at heart.)

The etymology makes schoolchildren drop their spinners and break into the giggles whenever they find in their readers sentences like, "When Reginald returned to the manor he had about him a queer look." Or, "The evening turned out to be so gay that Priscilla wished it should never end." Or, "Trevor awoke feeling a bit queer, but as the day wore on he was gay again."

I have at times described my E.W. as a "Latina" and I have heard her identify herself that way. "Chicana" used to be acceptable, but that word was coined during the political turmoils of the 1960s by Latinos who wanted to set themselves apart as a political force. Too many Latinos did not want to identify with some of the Chicanos' radical ideas, and so the term has fallen out of use. "Hispanic" is widely used, but strictly speaking it refers to someone whose heritage is of a Spanish-speaking country, and that covers a wide range of cultures and races. "Mexican-American" is fine, if the person really is a Mexican-American. He might be a Guatemalan-American.

Looking to the East, please note that "Oriental" is severely out, even though the word has never been shouted in anger or spoken out of hatred. It's hard to see how it became an insult, unless it's because the word referred to Eastern Asia and most folks are from the rest of Asia and don't want to be lumped in with that other crowd. Those who insist on using the word say it refers to anything or anyone Asian, or maybe only Chinese. In any case, it's not accurate in identifying a race or ethnic culture. So let's just not use that word unless we're referring to a rug. Our last normal president directed that it should not be used in official government documents. (The radical state of Washington beat him to it.) "Asian," it is. Asia, however, is a big hunk of the world and I'm not sure that everyone born in Asia fits the description, as we are supposed to understand it. Ah, diversity.

As for my lot, I'm okay with Caucasian or "white folks" or even European-American. But no black girl ever said, "You know the guy, works at the loading dock. European-American dude." Most of us will not take offense even at "honky" or "cracker." Having always been advantaged in America we can afford to be gracious in accepting whatever anyone else wants to call us. Still, "white devil" makes me a tad uncomfortable.

Now comes what this is all about. I have been around long enough to hear all the early slurs used freely to label a Negro, which itself is no longer in use, though once it was a term acceptable to everyone, including Martin Luther King. Those slurs were mean and hateful and I'm glad that only a small basket of deplorables never got the memo, or could read it if they did. (It is wishful thinking to say the basket is small.)

"Colored people" was once acceptable. (See the National Association for the Advancement of Colored People) And who doesn't love Lou Reed's riff, "And the colored girls go, doo do do do doo do do do doo..." (See "I Feel Funny Telling Colored Girls My Name is Darryl, Part One.") Now it's "people of color." Okay, I'll go along with it, but that includes everybody who isn't white. (Including my E.W., who is cinnamon, a skin tone celebrated in a great old song in the always understated ranchero style: "Ojos negros, piel canela/ que me llehan a desesperar," which translates to, "Black eyes, cinnamon skin/that drive me to desperation." I wish I had written that.)

Out of the social upheavals of the 1960s came the demand that a whole race of people would henceforth be called "blacks." (Most of all this changing of labels came out of the '60s. I was there. You could hardly keep up.) I remember at the time being happy to have it settled, once and for all, even though not all blacks were black. But I signed on and was comfortable saying something like, "You know who I mean, tall black dude, plays the alto sax."

Then out of the blue another shift occurred and the powers that were decided "black" was out and it should now be "African-American." People ought to be called what they want to be called, let me repeat, and I honor that, but this one doesn't make sense to me. A number of African-Americans would have to go back way far to find any connection to Africa and by that time I'm a member of the tribe myself. So are we all. And what do you call an Ethiopian dude from Paris teaching Spanish literature at Brown University? I make it easy on myself and go with "black." No one has taken offense yet, but the whole thing is a minefield. Let me apologize now and get it over with.

I know that writing about all this in a less-than-journalistic way runs the risk of my being called racist, mostly by honkies. What does someone desire when he calls someone else a racist? That the offender will retreat into some heavy introspection, maybe. I've already done that. Should I say something stupid out of ignorance or carelessness, I hope that the transgression be measured against my firmly held belief that nothing I have in life should ever be denied to anyone else because of a different heritage. You got a problem with that?

Which finally brings me to the pith of all this, an incident I have mined before in fiction, but here I tell the truth and nothing but the truth. It's instructive.

As earlier narrated, when I arrived in Los Angeles in 1965 I took the civil-service exam and became a social worker. I was not long out of the Navy and had driven alone across the country to find my place in the world. Three weeks after my orientation period the Watts Riots broke out. It was a terrible time.

Most of my colleagues, and my boss, were black women, and even though the streets were hot with racial tension we were all at ease with each other. We social workers sat at desks in orderly rows in a huge hall, fielding calls, dictating notes, or hanging out until taking to the field for an interview with an applicant. I sat next to Rhonda, a pleasant, outgoing black woman maybe a year or two younger than I. I didn't know her well but she seemed always of good humor. One day I told her my story and asked her how she became a social worker. Rhonda told me she used to be a transcriber, one of a legion of women who would take our dictation tapes and type them out for our case folders. She took night classes at Cal State and eventually got her degree. She came back to the same building where she used to work as a transcriber, this time as a professional, a social worker.

I congratulated her on her hard work and determination and said, "You know what we used to call you people in the Navy?"

She stiffened and gave me an icy stare. Her attitude changed completely.

"You people?" she said, a hard edge to her voice.

I knew I'd stepped on a mine. Since I couldn't see it I had no way of avoiding it.

"Yeah," I said, "people who work their way through the enlisted ranks and become officers. We called them mustangs. So in the Navy you'd be a mustang."

The ice melted and the warmth returned. She gave me a big smile.

I told Manzo, my roommate in that inner-city boarding house, about my exchange with Rhonda, how I screwed up somehow and that it confused me. He told me never to say "you people" to a black person. He couldn't say exactly why. It was some kind of collective hurtful memory of the soul.

The next day I went face to face with Rhonda and implored her to say something to me using that same offensive term. I wanted to give her the chance to get even but more than that I wanted to know what it felt like.

She thought about it for a moment, then said, "You people don't know how to make a good time out of nothing." I felt belittled. I wasn't one of a people who didn't know how to have a good time out of nothing. Was I? She laughed and gave me a hug and told me to snap out of it.

I never used the term "you people" again.

POSTSCRIPT:

Currently a new word has become controversial when used in reference to a black person. It is a dog whistle, they say, that only those tuned into subtle prejudices can hear it and know its intent. The word is "articulate." At the beginning of the controversy I thought, c'mon, "articulate" is a compliment in any context. Then I heard a black journalist say that he polled every black person he knew and they all agreed that "articulate" ticks them off. It's a passive-aggressive way of telling a single individual that he is a credit to his race. I had no idea. It didn't change my belief that "articulate" was one more explosive device that needn't be planted. Chill, bro. Take the compliment and move on.

I was interested enough, however, to delve into my own memory to find when and how I might have used that word in the past. I remembered only one incident, and I wasn't the one doing the talking at the time. I was in the office of a publicist I had for a book in 1975, listening to him speak on the phone. He was trying to set up interviews for me with the media. I heard him say, "You'll get a good interview. Ponicsán is good-looking and he's articulate." At the time I thought, yeah, I know that, but it was nice hearing someone else say it. Now all these years later I understand what he was saying. "For a scribe..."

The (SCRIPT) DOCTOR *IS IN*

The practice of making movies entertains the notion that two writers are better than one, so it would follow that three are better than two. In the process of getting a script into production several writers are often called upon to work either in concert or sequentially on the same story. This is unique in the field of creative writing.

Much of what I do is to take a script on which at least one other writer has already exhausted his resources. I grab the baton, usually from his unwilling hand, and try to carry the script over the finish line. I use what I can of what is good in the script but perhaps is misaligned or awkwardly executed. I bring what I can of my skills and life's experiences.

It happens like this: a producer is disappointed in the latest draft of a script that he and a studio and maybe a director are still keen on but are beginning to forget why. They agree that the idea is worth one more try by a different writer. I never know why they decided on me, but I can assume it's because they've looked at my past patients, even those that have died. It doesn't hurt to have a reputation for being fast, either, that reputation hard earned by working more and lunching less.

The producer talks to my agent, who talks to me about the players and the general background of the story. I am open to anything but superheroes, comic books, slasher pictures, gang rapes, and stories that pivot around one or more automobiles. Life's too short.

For years now most of what comes to me has "interest from Tom Cruise," who got his big break in a script I wrote called *Taps*, about boys in a military school. Someone might think we're friends or that he owes me a favor, but I haven't seen him since 1981 when he was in the habit of calling me "Sir," and he doesn't owe anything to me.

The latest draft of the troubled script is FedExed to me and I read it as soon as I open the envelope. Sometimes I can't get through it. A terminal case. Those that I read through I'll read a second time. I look for a seriousness of purpose and one good character.

Recognizing what is wrong with a script is easy and almost anyone can do it, though clearly articulating the problem goes a long way toward solving it. The love story doesn't work because...The relationship with the father doesn't work because...Whose story is it? What does the protagonist want? What's standing in his way? What is this picture saying about life for this person in this place at this time? What is working in the script? What must be retained at all costs? What has already been done to death in other movies?

I discuss these questions with the producer on the phone and usually again in person, this time with several other people in the room, people I don't know who nod enthusiastically.

Then I lay out how I would fix the thing. If they continue to nod I am going to get the job. My big secret for dealing with a sick script, apart from a medicine bag of cures gathered from years in my laboratory, is this: I put myself in the picture, in every frame. I trust that I am not that much different from others of my species and what is right for me will likely prove right for most others. Doesn't always work. Still,

I resist making my characters do what I wouldn't do myself given the same circumstances.

It takes me anywhere from four weeks to two years to rewrite a script. After the producer and his significant others read my draft we meet again. They raise their objections; I defend my choices. Then I'll go home and spend another two weeks, or years, addressing their notes. Sometimes an amazing thing happens. Despite their suggestions, the script is substantially improved.

I send in the revisions and one of two things occurs. One, I become a hero. I am kissed on all cheeks, congratulatory notes go into the dossier, and my fee goes up. Or, two, I become one more writer who couldn't lick it. On to the next writer for them, on to the next script for me.

Once I received a script from a producer with a note. *Everybody loves this script but there is something fundamentally wrong in the second act. Can you find out what, like right away, and fix it in two weeks?* It was a script I wrote four years before. Physician, heal thyself.

POSTSCRIPT:

You've watched the credits scroll by at the end of a movie and laughed as you counted off the number of producers and production companies. At least I have. How is it possible to have fifteen producers on a single picture? A producer's credit can be a reward or bargaining chip for moving the process one step further. For example, a producer needs a particular star who is hard to get. The star has a sidekick, a best friend from back when he was a nobody, one of the few people whose word he takes. The producer meets with the friend and promises him certain considerations and a producer's credit if he can bag the movie star. Sometimes the friend will get a credit even if he fails to convince his friend to star, if the movie is made with another star. The Writers Guild, on the other hand, does not allow a credit to every writer who worked on a particular script, though there may have been as many writers as there were producers. They believe, correctly, that it is uncomely and diminishes the art of film. The Guild limits the writing credits to three, four if one of them is a team. For example: "Written by A., B&C, and D."

Here's how they arrive at who gets credit: All of the drafts by all of the writers are submitted to the Guild, which impanels three volunteers from its rank and file to read them and decide who did what. This comes after the producer has submitted initial writing credits as he sees them. If any one of the writers denied credit objects he can call for an arbitration. The writers and the arbitrators are anonymous during the difficult process. A detailed schematic guides the arbitrators. It involves a formula of percentages contributed by each writer, too involved to explain in a postscript, and it may have already changed since the last time I was in arbitration.

In addition to determining credit the arbitrators must decide whose name comes first in the credits, the assumption being that the first credited writer contributed most. A first position might also mean that he wrote the original script and on that basis alone rates the first position. Personally, I prefer being second if there were two writers, third if three, because that means I was the one who brought it home. Credit is important to a writer not only for his filmography and his career going forward but for the residual that is paid four times a year. Years after a movie's release a residual might buy you a decent lunch. I know a writer, however, a serious writer and an Oscar winner, who was talked into doing the third or fourth sequel to a superhero movie. His first residual check was for $800,000.

A PRIMER ON *HOW TO END* YOUR LETTER *TO* NEWSPAPERS *with small CIRCULATIONS*

Those of us who still read newspapers and are of a certain age are drawn to the obituaries where we position ourselves in the grim continuum. Enough has been written by others about that shared experience already. I am more drawn to the opinion page where people old enough to be on the other page get things off their chests and pepper spray the reader with outrage, one surplus in America that everyone is willing to share. Attempts at bitter humor are made and fail, logic is lapsed or twisted, any originality is either unavailable to the writer or avoided, and it all ends in one of fifteen shrill rallying calls punctuated by one or more exclamation points and the odd word fortified by caps.

(All examples taken from actual letters to the editor)

"Have we all lost our minds!?"

"Wake UP, people!"

"Oh, I know! The almighty dollar!"

"Shame on them!"

"To those who object, I say get a LIFE!"

"Two wrongs do not make a right!!"

"Come on, people, get with the program!"

"Throw the bums OUT!!!"

"Are we taxpayers really paying for this?!!"

"Please, people, give it a rest!"

"The time to wake up is NOW!!!"

"Yeah, right. Give me a break!"

"Something is wrong with this picture!"

"Does anyone see the IRONY here?!!"

"Enough is enough!"

I feel BAD ABOUT my ROLE MODELS

Meeting a girl at a swimming pool puts a dude at a disadvantage. (I met my E.W. on Malibu Beach. She was in a bikini. Took my breath away. I've been her slave ever since.)The first time I saw the girl with whom I would exchange my virginity we were in a public swimming pool. I'll call her Eileen. (Come on, Eileen, you know who I mean.)

I was just seventeen and she was fifteen. In those days I was a dead ringer for James Dean, who was at the height of his short career. Thanks to that resemblance I got away with a lot. Whatever cool I was faking, however, dissolved in the chlorinated water as I watched Eileen ascend the ladder to the concrete perimeter. The sight of her butt put me into a trance.

It would be embarrassing to follow her up the ladder and reveal my boney ass and skinny legs, but she was too lovely to lose. I caught up with her and said, "Are you going to dive? Off the high board?"

"No, why?"

"I thought we could do it together."

She laughed. "You look like James Dean."

"I know."

"Why together?" she asked.

"It would be our first adventure."

"You go and I'll watch."

I had never even jumped off that high board. I had never

even climbed up to it. Now, what choice did I have? I had her interested. I had to put up or give up.

My stomach roiled as I ascended the ladder. Up, up. No turning back. Though only seventeen, it was not the first time I did something foolishly dangerous to impress a girl. I flashed back to that time I went over the handlebars of my bike while going full speed down a hill of coal dust.

Out on the end of the board, tentatively testing its spring, the breeze up there chilling my wet self, I felt so alone. I looked down at that little beauty who smiled up at me and held her hands in the prayer position. A couple of braver kids were impatiently waiting behind me. What was it, thirty feet? Not so high. Oh, wait, that's like a three-story building. I could just jump. In shame, it would be.

All right, this was going to happen. Nothing fancy. Your basic dive, simple yet elegant. I took as light a spring as the board would allow me and sailed into the air. *Not bad! She is mine!* Then I sensed my feet arcing forward and I couldn't stop the inevitable loop. Instead of watching the water I saw the sky. I landed flat on my back. It felt like a hundred lashes compressed into one incredibly cruel whack. I stayed underwater for as long as my whimpering lungs would allow.

I surfaced near the ladder. Eileen was standing there laughing. She reached down. I took her hand. "I'm all right." All right? I was in love. We talked for a few minutes, mostly about how insane I was, before she went to rejoin her friends. I told her I was going to return to the pool every day. Which of those days might she be there?

My role models when I was seventeen were James Dean, a troubled youth; Marlon Brando, a beast; and Mike Hammer, a callous private eye. All that I knew about women, I learned from them. Clearly bad choices, but no information was forthcoming from any other source. Certainly not from my mother, and I had no sisters. I had friends and classmates but those girls played it close to the blouse, as was the norm in those repressive Eisenhower years. Where I lived the older men were poor candidates to shape an adolescent in matters of romance, and my father avoided serious conversations, or conversations of any sort.

Whatever, Eileen and I became a couple. We were going steady.

Pity poor Eileen. I might pull her close to me, kiss her hard on the neck, and push her away, as Brando did to Mary Murphy in *The Wild One,* a movie that had a profound effect upon the adolescent me.

Pity poor Eileen. I once dropped her off from a date at her back door in the alley. As she walked away I rolled down the window of my '47 Chevy and said, "Show me your legs."

"What?"

"I want to see your legs."

The line came from Mike Hammer out of a hardboiled Mickey Spillane novel.

Eileen cocked her head to one side, confused but not inclined to investigate the source of her boyfriend's odd demand. She hiked up her skirt and looked at me like, happy now? WHAT WAS THE NEXT LINE? I couldn't remember. How was this scene supposed to end! I did what everyone who can't remember what to say does. I smiled and got away with it. She dropped her skirt and walked to the door.

It's hard to believe that sort of role playing worked, but not long after we sacrificed our virginity to each other, I far more enthusiastically than she, but equally as scared.

The magic moment unfolded in a cemetery, a good place for "parking," which was synonymous with making out in those days. I will omit the details of this intimate passage because it's possible Eileen may still be alive. I mean, *I'm* alive. I remember it, though, as full of anxiety, with no turning back. Like off the high-diving board.

That night the face in the mirror looking back at me was not my own and it took some days to accept the new one. The boy's face was gone forever, and at times I missed it, which is why I advise youngsters of all genders not to rush into the whole sex thing, and when it happens don't let it involve drugs, alcohol, or a cell phone. Look forward to it, make it memorably romantic.

POSTSCRIPT:

I once met John Paxton, the screenwriter of *The Wild One*, and I told him I had a crush on Mary Murphy, the lead actress, without telling him that I felt bad that Brando was once my role model. He said if I had met Mary Murphy back then I wouldn't have had a crush on her. I didn't ask why. I've been on the other side of that confession a few times and had to burst a young dude's passion for one or another actress short of the power to make anyone happy without a script. Paxton would have been a much better model himself, now that I think of it. One day when his wife returned home from errands, he got to his feet and said, "I'm dying. It's been a good life. I love you." And then he dropped dead.

I'll tell you who doesn't feel bad about her neck or his dick. Your dog.

As I understand it, and it's my guess I understand it about as well as anyone, Existentialism is a philosophy that requires its adherents to stake out personal freedom in any situation. Physical restraints vis-á-vis personal freedom is not a problem seeking a solution. It is the way humans *are,* though Existentialism is better appreciated by studying dogs.

A dog readily accepts what befalls him and goes for whatever he was going for before. A dog becomes whatever situation he finds himself in. He can lose a leg, for example, and pay hardly any attention to its loss. It is simply his new condition, readily accepted and easily forgotten. Should a tennis ball be thrown for him, an amputee dog doesn't hesitate, thinking, wait a minute, I have only three legs. He chases the ball. If a man, on the other hand, losses a leg—or the other hand—it becomes the focus of his life for as many years as he has left.

My dog Toby does a handstand, face deep into his bowl, and eats while balanced on his forepaws. Astonishing! I want to call out to someone, to verify that I can believe my own eyes. To Toby it's no big deal, it's merely how he feels about dinner this time. Later, I tell my friends about the phenomenon, but no one believes me. They don't say so, they only smile and talk about something else.

Someday, I am sure, Toby will speak like a dude, and his first word will be, "No," correcting some gauche behavior on my part. At this moment, as I type, he sits upon my lap, as is his due. Eventually he will lick my chin, signaling that it is time I stop my nonsense and take him to play with Max, the neighbor's Labrador.

For those brief periods during which I did not share my life with a dog—college, the Navy, grieving the loss of the last one—I felt like a man who had lost the path.

The dyslexic believes in Dog, and so do I. Blessed be we.

Man can teach Dog nothing of any significance. Dog knows. Dog is always correct. What man painstakingly practices to attain, Dog already has in spades. He is detached from ego, he accepts what is, every response he makes is the right one—fear, fight, flight, and forget—and he enjoys a good night's sleep after all.

Dog has a presence online but he blogs not, neither doth he manage a website. Rain does not stop Dog, nor does sun encourage him. Dog has no standard of beauty. Man drips with gold and subjects himself to bearing a stranger's name, say Tommy Hilfiger. Dog might wear a simple collar, because it seems to please people and he can't take it off anyway. Dog doesn't know or care when man is naked. The rarest and most exotic of breeds is just another mutt when Dog encounters him in the park.

For Dog the journey is the destination. When he jumps into the car, he doesn't know or care if he is going to Charlie's house or to Chicago, to the park or to Panama. He need not know how long he will be gone. He need not pack for the occasion. How I aspire to be like Dog! How certain I am that I will fail.

Dog is a carnivore without explaining why. He farts in

public without apology. He pukes wherever he wants to, including your bed, and then wonders why that should upset you. Man walks behind Dog on First Avenue and picks up his droppings in blue plastic bags. Down by the lake Dog rubs his neck, which he never feels bad about, in goose shit and then looks at you curiously while you wail. *I'm covering my scent, you moron!* he seems to say.

I sit on my porch reading the evening newspaper, bourbon and branch on the armrest. Dog's nose twitches almost imperceptibly, and he gets all the news that's fit to print. Hold the bourbon, pour the branch.

All hail Dog! Truly, Dog is great. On the overstuffed sofa of life, who could possibly sit above Dog?

Cat.

I *feel* BAD *ABOUT* MOM

Not mine, but all those moms who wind up in heartfelt books self-published by would-be writers who believe Mom was really something and their relationship special, for better or worse, and everyone should read about it.

Memoirs have long been considered commercially attractive by publishers, who urge celebrities to write one or to have someone write one for them. These books sell well and inspire ordinary people to foist upon their friends both real and virtual the story of how grandma came to America via Ellis Island with two hundred dollars to her name, which they changed for her. Her name, not the currency.

Mom memoirs have become a genre in their own right, with their own year's end lists: *10 Best, 15 Most Powerful, Must-Read, Most Hilarious, Most Heartwarming.* A few dad memoirs do exist, but neither women nor dudes are inclined in great numbers to share their relationship with dad unless as an exorcism. Even celebrities seem to steer clear of writing about Dad.

My own mom is long gone and we didn't have much of a relationship anyway. My father may have been a tad more demonstrative, though I have no valid evidence to cite. In their own way, I'm sure, they loved me, but their way was not to show it and not to talk about it. My father waited until his deathbed to say, "I love you, too." I don't recall my mother ever saying it, but I was not present at her passing. I was riding my Harley through freezing rain from Butte to Seattle and I arrived at her bedside a little late. Neither one of them ever gave me a "Good job!" like parents do today, even to twelve-year-olds who pick up their shoes, around the age at which I was picking unburned coal out of tubs of ashes and truly doing a good job. I might have copped a hug from one of them but can't remember any before I became an adult and would show up for a visit after an absence of a year or two. They didn't want their kids to be soft or full of themselves or even in the house that much.

As a child I always had a roof over my head and three meals a day, at least one of which was unwanted and forced upon me before I could take to the streets. I lived in a congenial but risky neighborhood. The feel of caked blood in my hair was familiar to me. I played with friends being raised in a similar fashion. In college I learned an expression which I could charitably apply to my upbringing: "laissez faire."

When I was eight my mom gifted me with two pairs of boxing gloves. The second pair was to be lent to some other kid before we set about pummeling each other. It was her plan to foster toughness, but I know she found it entertaining.

At that age I got a job setting pins at the bowling alley behind our house, picking up and smoking smoldering cigars left in ashtrays, and working well beyond the bedtime of a normal eight-year-old.

"Where's Darryl?"

"Don't know. Haven't seen him since breakfast."

"Ronnie, go to the bowling alley. Remind him to come home."

All in all, I had a happy childhood in an area where at first glance that might not be expected. My parents provided me a comfortable if precarious home, a row house sitting atop a working mine, and they fed me well. They eventually bought a freestanding house on a solid foundation for $9,000 and took out a second mortgage on it in order to put me through college. My father's idea. I thought it would be a waste of money.

I never had more than a few serious conversations with either one of them, few and far between, and brief.

As an example, around ten years of age I came to realize that death was inescapable no matter how good a boy you were and it lasted a long time. Panicked, I told Mom I didn't want to die. She said, "A good Lutheran doesn't worry about dying." The conundrum that created in a ten-year-old's mind and his dealing with it as he went through life would fill another book twice this long.

Seven years later, home from my first year of college, we engaged in another serious conversation, my confession that I got a tattoo. I had hid it for months in long sleeves because in those days only ex-cons and sailors had tattoos. I approached her in the kitchen where she was frying bleenies and uneasily said I had something to tell her. She never put down the spatula, and I could see she didn't want to hear it. I finally rolled up my sleeve, and displayed the pathetic thing: my first name bordered by two stars, applied by Sailor Bill at the Allentown State Fair.

She looked it over and said, "This could come in handy."

"Really?"

"You might be in a strange city somewhere and wake up and not know who you are, so you look at your arm…"

I was unsettled by her response. I was prepared for her to point out how stupid I was. Instead her words forced me to envision myself awakening in a hotel room and not having any idea who I was, a scenario hard to scrub from your daydreams. A few days later she admitted she was relieved to see my anxiety was from nothing more than a tattoo. "I thought you were going to tell me you got some girl pregnant."

I had had sex only once and came out not entirely unscathed but fortunately another thirteen years from paternity.

Eighteen and entering my sophomore year of college, with everyone inquiring about what plan I had for my future, I had another serious word with her, again in the kitchen.

"I decided what I want to do," I said.

"What?"

"I want to be a writer," I said.

"How can you be a writer? You've never been anywhere."

She went back to prepping blind pigeons for dinner.

For years I thought it was the wrong thing for a mother to say to her son, but later I came to believe that discouragement is good for a young person who wants to be a writer. I've helped others in that way myself. When I sent her a copy of my first novel and then called from Los Angeles to ask her if she liked it, she said, "I liked the cover."

"I'll pass that on to the graphic artist."

This makes her sound hard, I know, but she had her moments and was more sympathetic in her infrequent letters to me after I left home. When I was going through a nasty divorce she wrote, *"You took a long time building your character. Don't let this crack it."* Good advice, and coming from her, touching, though by then I had already suffered a couple cracks in my character. They fill in, but it takes years.

POSTSCRIPT:

When I was fifty and no less worried that I might wake up in a hotel room not knowing my name, I redid my teenage tattoo with something more assertive. By that time tattoos had gone mainstream. I opted for a Japanese catfish leaping out of a suggested lake. I was told that in Japan the catfish is a harbinger of the earthquake, and I always pass that on to people who ask, adding that if that catfish on my arm starts wiggling, drop under a table.

A bleenie, by the way, is much like the Jewish latke but thinner because the potatoes are more finely grated.

A blind pigeon? Ground beef and rice rolled in a cabbage leaf and baked in tomato sauce.

THERE *is* NO *ALTERNATIVE*
or
IT is WHAT *IT is*
or
EVERYTHING *IS COPY*
(But You Don't Have to Write It) (And I Don't Have to Read It)

I've always had a dog or two or three. When I became a senior citizen I thought it sensible to rescue dogs who were also senior citizens, dogs with less time in front of them than behind them, like me. One of them was a snarky little Pomeranian mutt named Gizmo, a "hospice" dog with only weeks left. He joined the two old dogs I already had, Toby, a Jack Russell boy; and Sheba, a Chihuahua girl, paying them scant attention and making the best of his new situation. Like many rescue dogs traumatized by abandonment and cruelty, he didn't know how to play or even to express any emotions. In time he became happy to see me come home, but the only way he knew to show it was to push the side of his face along the carpet. He lived with us for eighteen months, outlasting Toby, and in his own way was happy.

Watching them decline, dog after dog, I had to go through the grim process of determining when they should be put down. I remember once digging a grave in the back yard for my yellow Lab, Blondie, who had a day or two left, I determined. Cleaning up dishes at the kitchen sink, I looked outside and saw Blondie peering down into her own open grave. She caught a second wind, and held on for another six weeks.

The doggy decline, like its master's, usually begins with something small. A cough, a limp, a stumble, a lump. Off to the vet, some pills, let's keep an eye on him. Then something else would take a bad turn, and still another thing, piling up, and then the original thing got worse and it became clear that my dog was near the end of his downward spiral.

These days I look upon myself in much the same way. I am not the dog I used to be, even a year ago. (A long time in a dog's life, not so long in mine.) Little annoyances become issues. Feet, knees, hips, back, jaw, neck, dick. Hearing loss, eyes full of darting fruit flies, debilitating allergies, violent sneezing, shortness of breath, bursitis, low thyroid, inflammation—no one thing that by itself could kill me, but in concert soften me up for the final blow, the new hell lurking over my left shoulder.

I dread the night, and each one comes sooner than the last. The ritual of getting ready for bed grows longer, bringing memories of when all I had to do was take off my clothes and roll under the covers. Likewise, mornings require more of me and offer less in return. Waking up is like opening a grab-bag at a traveling carnival. I know that it will not be a treasure but maybe it won't be too cheesy.

My longest-lasting friendship is with my former college roommate. For over fifty years we've lived on opposite coasts, so we don't see each other any more, relying on email for updates. We share the same disease. He's had the worst of it, having lost two organs and incidentally replacing a couple joints with hardware. He tells his wife he's leaving her, one piece at a time. He is a year older than I, and our birthdays are a few weeks apart. I emailed him when he hit eighty and gave him a virtual high-five. He told me that everybody gives him hugs now and calls him handsome. Young women open doors for him. People smile and describe him as "eighty years young." He wants to smack them. Live long enough and you will enter into that part of your Golden Years that is neither golden nor years, when a stomachache is something far different for you than for a dude in his twenties. Sometimes I feel stuck in Lodi again even though I've never been there before.

Most of this rude awakening comes after everything in pop culture has already become irrelevant. I no longer have to deal with an overbearing boss, nor a venal landlord, nor a sloppy roommate, nor a spacey girlfriend, nor a shit job, nor an annoying co-worker. When I watch sitcoms in which circles of young friends get into hilarious situations, I might as well be looking through an interstellar telescope. On the other hand, with age one loses the condition so prevalent among the young: FOBLO, in their lexicon; fear of being left out, in mine.

In her book Nora confessed to being in denial on the subject of death. She is not the only one. Every time I go in for a surgery my E.W. says, "You're going to be fine." Like she knows. It doesn't take a casino pit boss to see she's blowing on the dice. I try to follow the example of Dog. Dog doesn't know he is going to die. He's not aware of time passing or growing old. Whatever befalls him he accepts and carries on, day by day. Dog plays it as it lays. Easy enough for him, he has nothing to look forward to besides dinner and a walk.

I had two books and a movie scheduled for release. I had to hang on. Taken with my first novel in 1970 and my first movie in 1973 they would bring my career full circle so of course I wanted to be alive to see that happen and bask in the satisfaction of it.

It is a staple of comedy that whenever two old people get together the conversation quickly turns to meds and surgeries. I see no way around setting up that threadbare skit here. It is, after all, where all of this leads, and when I say "all of this" I mean *all* of this. If it's not one thing, it's your mother.

Remember, "What doesn't kill me makes me stronger"? That's bullshit. Mottos like that may help when you're a tough dude in your twenties, getting stitched up after some misadventure, but an old man doesn't get stronger. The best he can hope for is to survive until the next thing and maybe it will be quick and painless.

Yes, Miss, I do have an "Advance Health Care Directive," and it does include my Choice Not to Prolong Life. It's in a thick three-ring binder my estate planner concocted.The binder includes my handwritten instructions to avoid the kind of ritual I attended often enough growing up, when the dearly departed was laid out downstairs in the parlor, on display for friends and neighbors, welcome to drop in, have a shot and a beer, and comment on how good Leo looks in his coffin, props to the undertaker, good job. These instructions were written ten years ago, so I asked, "Can I add something about keeping me alive until my movie comes out?" If it looks like it might be a success, keep me going long enough to enjoy it, maybe until I receive an Oscar, where I will forego any wit or gushing gratitude and instead take a knee on national TV and count on my co-writer helping me get to my feet again. If the movie is going to tank, however, please pull the plug. (It tanked, but there was no plug to pull. So let's say, as L'il Kim might, "It's all good.")

A friend has told his wife that he would prefer not to involve her in his death in any way, shape, or manner, for her own good, to make it easier for her to begin a new life without him. To prepare for that event required some detailed orchestration on his part and blind trust on his wife's part. He has given her a phone number to enter into all her devices and to carry in her purse. Upon his death all she has to do is call that number. A man in a dark suit will come right over to the house or the hospital or wherever and remove his corpse from the premises, dispose of it properly and neither the remains of my friend nor the man in the dark suit will ever be seen again. All paid for in advance. This is not a comfort to his wife. It is, however, a comfort to my friend, and though I would not emulate his idea, I get it.

My instructions, knowing full well that it won't matter whether they are followed or not, are that this raft I've been on should anchor wherever it lands for a period of at least four hours, during which time some doo-wop should be played. The Platters, the Penguins, the Cadillacs, the Drifters, and also the girl groups: the Crystals, the Marvelettes, the Supremes, the Shirelles, Martha and the Vandellas. The four hours, I read somewhere, make it a smooth transition to the next life if reincarnation is a thing. No funeral is to be staged, but should anyone want to host a memorial then I would like a reading of "Spring and Fall: To a Young Child" a poem by Gerard Manley Hopkins, to remind all in attendance that they are not in this alone. (This is a difficult poem to read aloud and I am still mentally auditioning who might best pull it off. I may have to record it myself.) As for ceremonial music, "Telstar" by the Tornados, as everyone lifts a glass and calls good-bye. Food, drink, talk, whatever; I leave that to my heirs. The guest of honor will have had a previous obligation. Regrets.

I've had twelve surgeries over fourteen years, in the same place for the same reason. They've become routine. Before the last one, Dr. Dark paid a courtesy call and said, "This ought to be a chip shot." Moments later they wheeled me to the OR and set me on a tee.

Coming to and having it all in the past is always a pleasant surprise, except when a nurse shows up in a hazmat suit. But then it's not long before I'm pushed into the sunlight by a cheery volunteer and sent on my way, albeit with a bag strapped to my leg, to recuperate at home before six weeks more of chemo, the easy kind, pumped right to the source. No loss of hair. So there's that. More treatments are scheduled for the fall and the following spring, provided I am still here to receive them. When told that my future would be punctuated by these assaults I asked what would happen if I chose to do nothing, the basic dude default. Dr. Dark said, "It could get real ugly." I did not imagine it would be pretty.

Three times a year he sends a periscope all up in there to look for invaders. It is a humbling experience, ask anyone. During one of those explorations he will find one or two advance scouts and I'm off to the hospital again where he sends a laser with a night scope up the same path to zap whatever might be taking cover, and I experience once again the dress rehearsal for death, the void of general anesthesia during which no difference can be made between an hour or a century. Then it's six more weeks of toxic chemicals following the same route, up little Donny. A monotone nurse does this while wearing a full face mask and hazmat suit because the solution contains the tuberculosis virus and you don't want that stuff splashing around. At the end of six weeks I give her a couple bottles of fine wine and say, see you down the road.

If the reader is still with me she might be hoping that, as tacitly promised, all this arrives somewhere. It does, to a new perspective and an unexpected outro to this warble in the key of B Minor.

The new perspective: I feel bad about my dick? Shut up. My dick feels bad about *me.*

The unexpected outro: No matter how many eyes an old potato may have, it still can't see in the dark.

CHAPTERS *that* DID NOT *make the* CUT

Releasing the Feminine Me: It's Not Pretty

My Low Thyroid (Or: I Feel Bad About My Neck)

The Eighth Deadly Sin

I Feel Bad About My *Knees*!

I Feel Funny Telling Colored Girls My Name is Darryl (Part Two)

Most People Want to be Gladys Knight, But I Want to Be a Pip

I Feel Bad About My Face (Look Away!)

The Eighth Wonder of the World

How to Default on a Karmic Debt

Will Quinn the Eskimo Ever Get Here?

Diary of a Last Responder

I Feel Bad About My Chin!

I Feel Bad? About Upspeakers?
I Can't Figure Out Why They Do That?

The Eighth Pillar of Wisdom

When Two Names Are Not Enough
(I'm Talking About You, Mary Louise Parker)

Ten Things I've Always Known (But Chose to Forget)

On Rupture

I Feel Bad About My Pad, Part Two

The Story of the Other Half of My Life

AFTERWORD

Some of these observations appeared in different contexts in previous publications. "Ménage-á-What?", "Why It's Called a Waiting Room," and "I Feel Bad About the Odds" all debuted in *The Los Angeles Herald-Examiner*, where I was once Writer-in-Residence.

"As Dog Is My Witness" was published in *Tricycle*, a Buddhist quarterly.

"The (Script) Doctor Is In" was an answer to a request from the *Puget Sound Business Journal.*

A few lines here and there found their way out of my fiction. Everything is copy.

FINAL POSTSCRIPT

Since writing that last chapter, which even I will concede is a bit bleak, I find my general health has taken a dramatic turn for the better; credit to losing forty pounds nose to toes and four inches off my waist. An old man *can* get stronger, it seems. I brought a writer's discipline to the mission. I eat only real food and not too much of it. I wake up every morning at 5:30 and walk a mile and a half. In the course of personal events I'll tack on another four miles before going to bed at 9:30 and sleeping well, given my history. I practice Tai Chi and Qi Gong daily, take a somatic meditation break, work the cables, and swim more than the average dude my age. The last surgery was surprisingly easy and the nurse in the hazmat suit was not summoned. On a recent foray in, Dr. Dark found nada. Dr. Z. is amazed by my make-over. She told me that if I quit drinking I could be Batman. I'm getting a second opinion.

DARRYL PONICSÁN

is the author of fourteen novels and an award-winning screenwriter. Born in Shenandoah, Pa., he taught high school English after attending Muhlenberg College and earning an MA at Cornell University. This is his first non-fiction book.

Visit the author at:

www.darrylponicsan.com

www.ingramcontent.com/pod-product-compliance
Lightning Source LLC
Chambersburg PA
CBHW070323120726
47909CB00008B/2571